بـسم الله الرحمن الرحيم

TO THE READER

- In all the books by the author, faith-related issues are explained in the light of the Qur'anic verses and people are invited to learn God's words and to live by them. All the subjects that concern God's verses are explained in such a way as to leave no room for doubt or question marks in the reader's mind. The sincere, plain and fluent style employed ensures that everyone of every age and from every social group can easily understand the books. This effective and lucid narrative makes it possible to read them in a single sitting. Even those who rigorously reject spirituality are influenced by the facts recounted in these books and cannot refute the truthfulness of their contents.

- This book and all the other works of the author can be read individually or discussed in a group at a time of conversation. Those readers who are willing to profit from the books will find discussion very useful in the sense that they will be able to relate their own reflections and experiences to one another.

- In addition, it will be a great service to the religion to contribute to the presentation and reading of these books, which are written solely for the good pleasure of God. All the books of the author are extremely convincing. For this reason, for those who want to communicate the religion to other people, one of the most effective methods is to encourage them to read these books.

- It is hoped that the reader will take time to look through the review of other books on the final pages of the book, and appreciate the rich source of material on faith-related issues, which are very useful and a pleasure to read.

- In these books, you will not find, as in some other books, the personal views of the author, explanations based on dubious sources, styles that are unobservant of the respect and reverence due to sacred subjects, nor hopeless, doubt-creating, and pessimistic accounts that create deviations in the heart.

THE
MIRACLE
OF
CREATION
IN DNA

The Truth Revealed by the
Human Genome Project

HARUN YAHYA

Goodword Books

First published 2003
© Goodword Books 2003

Goodword Books Pvt. Ltd.
1, Nizamuddin West Market
New Delhi-110 013
Tel. 435 5454, 435 6666
Fax 9111-435 7333, 435 7980
e-mail: info@goodwordbooks.com
www.goodwordbooks.com

www.harunyahya.com
info@harunyahya.com

ABOUT THE AUTHOR

The author, who writes under the pen-name HARUN YAHYA, was born in Ankara in 1956. Having completed his primary and secondary education in Ankara, he then studied arts at Istanbul's Mimar Sinan University and philosophy at Istanbul University. Since the 1980s, the author has published many books on political, faith-related and scientific issues. Harun Yahya is well-known as an author who has written very important works disclosing the imposture of evolutionists, the invalidity of their claims and the dark liaisons between Darwinism and bloody ideologies such as fascism and communism.

His pen-name is made up of the names "Harun"(Aaron)and "Yahya"(John), in memory of the two esteemed prophets who fought against lack of faith. The Prophet's seal on the cover of the author's books has a symbolic meaning linked to the their contents. This seal represents the Qur'an, the last Book and the last word of God, and our Prophet, the last of all the prophets. Under the guidance of the Qur'an and Sunnah, the author makes it his main goal to disprove each one of the fundamental tenets of godless ideologies and to have the "last word", so as to completely silence the objections raised against religion. The seal of the Prophet, who attained ultimate wisdom and moral perfection, is used as a sign of his intention of saying this last word.

All these works by the author centre around one goal:to convey the message of the Qur'an to people, thus encouraging them to think about basic faith-related issues, such as the existence of God, His unity and the hereafter, and to display the decrepit foundations and perverted works of godless systems.

Harun Yahya enjoys a wide readership in many countries, from India to America, England to Indonesia, Poland to Bosnia, and Spain to Brazil. Some of his books are available in English, French, German, Italian, Spanish, Portuguese, Urdu, Arabic, Albanian, Russian, Serbo-Croat (Bosnian), Polish, Malay, Uygur Turkish, and Indonesian, and they have been enjoyed by readers all over the world.

Greatly appreciated all around the world, these works have been instrumental in many people putting their faith in God and in many others gaining a deeper insight into their faith. The wisdom, and the sincere and easy-to-understand style employed give these books a distinct touch which directly strikes any one who reads or examines them. Immune to objections, these works are characterised by their features of rapid effectiveness, definite results and irrefutability. It is unlikely that those who read these books and give a serious thought to them can any longer sincerely advocate the materialistic philosophy, atheism and any other perverted ideology or philosophy. Even if they continue to advocate, this will be only a sentimental insistence since these books have refuted these ideologies from their very basis. All contemporary movements of denial are ideologically defeated today, thanks to the collection of books written by Harun Yahya.

There is no doubt that these features result from the wisdom and lucidity of the Qur'an. The author certainly does not feel proud of himself;he merely intends to serve as a means in one's search for God's right path. Furthermore, no material gain is sought in the publication of these works.

Considering these facts, those who encourage people to read these books, which open the "eyes"of the heart and guide them in becoming more devoted servants of God, render an invaluable service.

Meanwhile, it would just be a waste of time and energy to propagate other books which create confusion in peoples'minds, lead man into ideological chaos, and which, clearly have no strong and precise effects in removing the doubts in peoples'hearts, as also verified from previous experience. It is apparent that it is impossible for books devised to emphasize the author's literary power rather than the noble goal of saving people from loss of faith, to have such a great effect. Those who doubt this can readily see that the sole aim of Harun Yahya's books is to overcome disbelief and to disseminate the moral values of the Qur'an. The success, impact and sincerity this service has attained are manifest in the reader's conviction.

One point needs to be kept in mind:The main reason for the continuing cruelty and conflict, and all the ordeals the majority of people undergo is the ideological prevalence of disbelief.

These things can only come to an end with the ideological defeat of disbelief and by ensuring that everybody knows about the wonders of creation and Qur'anic morality, so that people can live by it. Considering the state of the world today, which forces people into the downward spiral of violence, corruption and conflict, it is clear that this service has to be provided more speedily and effectively. Otherwise, it may be too late. It is no exaggeration to say that the collection of books by Harun Yahya have assumed this leading role. By the Will of God, these books will be the means through which people in the 21st century will attain the peace and bliss, justice and happiness promised in the Qur'an.

The works of the author include: *The New Masonic Order, Judaism and Freemasonry, Global Freemasonry, Islam Denounces Terrorism, Terrorism:The Devil's Ritual, The Disasters Darwinism Brought to Humanity, Communism in Ambush, Fascism:The Bloody Ideology of Darwinism, The 'Secret Hand'in Bosnia, Behind the Scenes of The Holocaust, Behind the Scenes of Terrorism, Israel's Kurdish Card, The Oppression Policy of Communist China and Eastern Turkestan, Palestine, Solution:The Values of the Qur'an, The Winter of Islam and Its Expected Spring, Articles 1-2-3, A Weapon of Satan: Romantism, Signs from the Chapter of the Cave to the Last Times, Signs of the Last Day, The Last Times and The Beast of the Earth, Truths 1-2, The Western World Turns to God, The Evolution Deceit, Precise answers to Evolutionists, The Blunders of Evolutionists, Confessions of Evolutionists, The Qur'an Denies Darwinism, Perished Nations, For Men of Understanding, The Prophet Moses, The Prophet Joseph, The Prophet Mohammed, The Prophet Solomon, The Golden Age, Allah's Artistry in Colour, Glory is Everywhere, The Importance of the Evidences of Creation, The Truth of the Life of This World, The Nightmare of Disbelief, Knowing the Truth, Eternity Has Already Begun, Timelessness and the Reality of Fate, Matter:Another Name for Illusion, The Little Man in the Tower, Islam and the Philosophy of Karma, The Dark Magic of Darwinism, The Religion of Darwinism, The Collapse of the Theory of Evolution in 20 Questions, Allah is Known Through Reason, The Qur'an Leads the Way to Science, The Real Origin of Life, Consciousness in the Cell, A String of Miracles, The Creation of the Universe, Miracles of the Qur'an, The Design in Nature, Self-Sacrifice and Intelligent Behaviour Models in Animals, The End of Darwinism, Deep Thinking, Never Plead Ignorance, The Green Miracle:Photosynthesis, The Miracle in the Cell, The Miracle in the Eye, The Miracle in the Spider, The Miracle in the Gnat, The Miracle in the Ant, The Miracle of the Immune System, The Miracle of Creation in Plants, The Miracle in the Atom, The Miracle in the Honeybee, The Miracle of Seed, The Miracle of Hormone, The Miracle of the Termite, The Miracle of the Human Body, The Miracle of Man's Creation, The Miracle of Protein, The Miracle of Smell and Taste, The Secrets of DNA.*

The author's childrens books are: *Wonders of Allah's Creation, The World of Animals, The Splendour in the Skies, Wonderful Creatures, Let's Learn Our Religion, The World of Our Little Friends: The Ants, Honeybees That Build Perfect Combs, Skillful Dam Builders: Beavers.*

The author's other works on Quranic topics include: *The Basic Concepts in the Qur'an, The Moral Values of the Qur'an, Quick Grasp of Faith 1-2-3, Ever Thought About the Truth?, Crude Understanding of Disbelief, Devoted to Allah, Abandoning the Society of Ignorance, The Real Home of Believers: Paradise, Knowledge of the Qur'an, Qur'an Index, Emigrating for the Cause of Allah, The Character of the Hypocrite in the Qur'an, The Secrets of the Hypocrite, The Names of Allah, Communicating the Message and Disputing in the Qur'an, Answers from the Qur'an, Death Resurrection Hell, The Struggle of the Messengers, The Avowed Enemy of Man:Satan, The Greatest Slander:Idolatry, The Religion of the Ignorant, The Arrogance of Satan, Prayer in the Qur'an, The Theory of Evolution, The Importance of Conscience in the Qur'an, The Day of Resurrection, Never Forget, Disregarded Judgements of the Qur'an, Human Characters in the Society of Ignorance, The Importance of Patience in the Qur'an, General Information from the Qur'an, The Mature Faith, Before You Regret, Our Messengers Say, The Mercy of Believers, The Fear of Allah, Jesus Will Return, Beauties Presented by the Qur'an for Life, A Bouquet of the Beauties of Allah 1-2-3-4, The Iniquity Called "Mockery, "The Mystery of the Test, The True Wisdom According to the Qur'an, The Struggle with the Religion of Irreligion, The School of Yusuf, The Alliance of the Good, Slanders Spread Against Muslims Throughout History, The Importance of Following the Good Word, Why Do You Deceive Yourself?, Islam:The Religion of Ease, Enthusiasm and Excitement in the Qur'an, Seeing Good in Everything, How do the Unwise Interpret the Qur'an?, Some Secrets of the Qur'an, The Courage of Believers, Being Hopeful in the Qur'an, Justice and Tolerance in the Qur'an, Basic Tenets of Islam, Those Who do not Listen to the Qur'an, Taking the Qur'an as a Guide, A Lurking Threat: Heedlessness, Sincerity in the Qur'an.*

CONTENTS

INTRODUCTION:
A MAJOR MILESTONE
IN THE HISTORY OF HUMANITY

Today is the day of a major milestone in history. The materialist philosophy, once imposed on the mass of humanity under the guise of science, is ironically being defeated today by science itself. Materialism, the philosophy which holds that everything is composed of matter and which denies the existence of God, is actually the contemporary version of paganism. Ancient pagans used to worship non-living beings like wooden or stone totem poles and considered them divine beings. Materialist philosophy, on the other hand, bases its claim on the belief that man and all other beings are created out of atoms and molecules. According to this superstitious view, non-living atoms somehow organised themselves and over time acquired life and consciousness, finally bringing man into being.

This superstitious belief based on materialism is called **"evolution."** The belief in evolution, first introduced in the pagan cultures of the ancient Sumerians and then the ancient Greeks, was in a way revived in the 19th century by a group of materialist scientists and brought on to the world agenda. Charles Darwin is the best known of these scientists. The theory of evolution he advanced wasted the time of the world of science for 150 years, and despite its flawed nature having been widely acknowledged, it has been sustained until quite recently for purely ideological reasons.

However, as mentioned earlier, today, materialism is collapsing with a resounding crash. It is often stated that there were three important materialist theorists who steered the 19th century: **Freud, Marx and Darwin.** The theories of the first two were examined, tested, and, proving

Charles Darwin　　　　　**Karl Marx**　　　　　**Sigmund Freud**

invalid, subsequently rejected in the 20th century. Nowadays, the theory of Darwin is also collapsing.

Some important developments in June 2000 accelerated this great downfall of materialism.

First, scientists carrying out experiments to break the speed of light made a discovery which turned all scientific premises upside down. In an experiment in which the speed of light was broken, the scientists observed with astonishment that **the effect of the experiment occurred before its cause.** This meant the defeat of the claim of **"causality"** that was put forward on the basis of materialist views in the 19th century. It was reported in many scientific publications that **"this experiment proved that effect without cause is possible and that the end of an event can happen before its beginning."** Indeed, the occurrence of the effect of an action before the action that seems to be its cause, is scientific evidence that all events are created individually. This totally demolishes the materialist dogma.

A few weeks later, it was revealed that **Archaeopteryx, a fossil bird presented as "the most important fossil evidence" by Darwinists for more than a century, was actually not evidence for, but a blow to the theory.** When another fossil, some 75 million years older than this fossil which was allegedly the "primitive ancestor of birds," and no different from modern birds, was discovered, evolutionists were shocked. **Many journals which used to present Archaeopteryx as the "primitive** ancestor of birds" were obliged to report that **"The Ancestor of Birds Proved to be a Bird."**

Finally, **the Human Genome Project**, an attempt to draft a rough map of the human genome, was concluded and **the details of the "genetic information," which highlighted how superior God's creation of living beings is, have been revealed to mankind.** Today, everyone who considers the results of this project and finds out that a single human cell contains enough information to be stored in thousands of encyclopaedia pages, grasps what a great miracle of creation this is.

Nevertheless, evolutionists try to misinterpret this recent development, which, in truth, works against them, and present it as evidence for "evolution." Unable to explain even how the DNA chain of a tiny bacterium originated, evolutionists try to deliver messages such as "human genes resemble animal genes." Such messages are inaccurate and have no scientific value. They are designed to mislead society. Meanwhile, some press institutions, both because of their ignorance on the subject and their prejudiced approach, suppose that the Human Genome Project provides "evidence of evolution" and try to present it that way.

In this book, the above-mentioned evolutionist misconceptions are explained and the irrational and shallow nature of the objections raised to creation is clarified. In addition, the severity of the blow to Darwinism struck by the recent findings is explicitly revealed.

When you read this book, you too will see that materialist philosophy which rejects God is about to meet its end and that in the 21st century, humanity will return to accepting the real purpose of their creation by being relieved of deceits such as evolution.

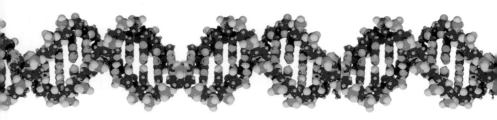

DNA:
THE DATA SOURCE OF LIFE

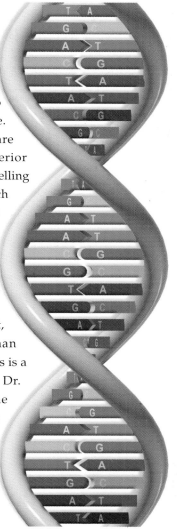

T he progress of science makes it clear that living beings have an extremely complex structure and an order too perfect to have come into being by coincidence. This is evidence to the fact that living beings are created by an All-Powerful Creator with superior knowledge. Recently, for instance, with the unravelling of the perfect structure in the human gene-which became a prominent issue due to the Genome Project-the unique creation of God has once more been revealed for all to see.

From the U.S.A. to China, scientists from all over the world have given their best efforts over a decade to decode the 3 billion chemical letters in DNA and to determine their sequence. As a result, 85% of the data included in the DNA of human beings could be properly sequenced. Although this is a very exciting and important development, as Dr. Francis Collins, who leads the Human Genome Project states, so far, only the first step has been taken in the decoding of the information in DNA.

In order to understand why the decoding of this information takes so long, we have to understand the nature of the information stored in DNA.

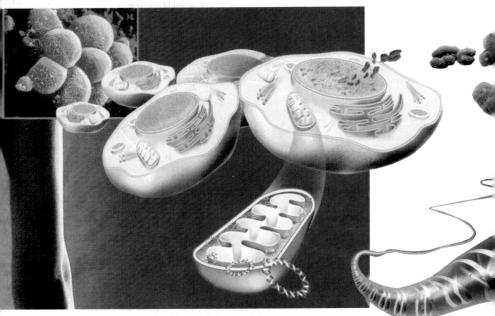

The Secret Structure of DNA

In the manufacture of a technological product or the management of a plant, the greatest tools employed are the experience and accumulation of knowledge that man has acquired over many centuries. The necessary knowledge and experience needed for the construction of the human body, the most advanced and sophisticated "plant" on earth, are stored in DNA. DNA is a rather large molecule that is carefully protected in the cell nucleus, and functions as a kind of data bank for the human body. The information hidden inside DNA controls the thousands of different events that take place in the cells of the human body and in the functioning of its systems, as well as all physical features, from the colour of a person's hair and eyes to his height. For example, even whether someone's blood pressure is high, low or normal depends on the information in DNA.

The important point that needs to be stressed here is that ever since the very first human being, the trillions of examples of DNA in the billions of human cells have been appearing in the same state of perfection and complexity as at present. As you read the lines below, you will also come to see how it is clearly unreasonable to claim, as evolutionists do, that such a molecule, with all its mind-blowing structure and properties, originated as a result of coincidences.

Volumes of Information in the Human Cell

The information stored in DNA must by no means be underestimated. So much so that one human DNA molecule contains enough information to fill a million-page encyclopaedia, or to fill about 1,000 books. Note this fact well: one million encyclopaedia pages, or 1,000 books. This is to say that the nucleus of each cell contains as much information as would fill a one-million-page encyclopaedia, which is used to control the functions of the human body. To draw an analogy, we can state that even the 23-volume-*Encyclopaedia Britannica*, one of the greatest mines of information in the world, has 25,000 pages. Therefore, before us lies an incredible picture. In a molecule found in a nucleus, which is far smaller than the microscopic cell wherein it is located, there exists a

There is enough information in one DNA molecule to fill 1,000 books. This is encoded in the DNA seen in the picture. All of a person's features are encoded in an alphabet symbolized in the letters A, T, C and G.

data warehouse 40 times bigger than the biggest encyclopaedia of the world that includes millions of items of information. This means a huge 1000-volume encyclopaedia which is unique and has no equal in the world. Were one piece of information present in human genes to be read every second, non-stop, around the clock, it would take 100 years to complete the process. If we imagine that the information in DNA were put into book form, the volumes placed on top of each other would reach 70 metres high. The latest calculations have revealed that this huge encyclopaedia contains some 3 billion different "subjects." If the information in DNA were to be written down on paper, that paper would stretch from the North Pole to Ecuador.

These examples are an indication of the imposing amount of information contained in DNA. Yet how can we talk of a molecule containing information? This is because what we talk about here is not a computer or a library, but just a piece of flesh that is a hundred thousand times smaller than a millimetre, simply made up of protein, fat and water molecules. It is a miracle of astounding proportions that this infinitesimal piece of flesh should contain and store even a single bit of information-let alone millions of bits.

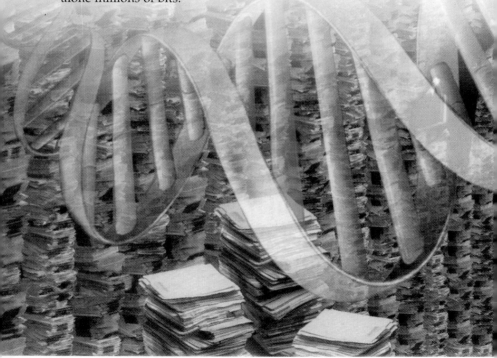

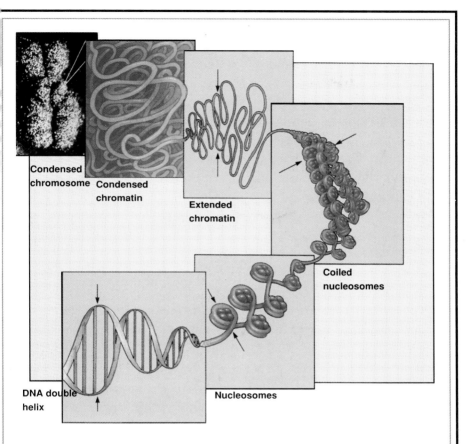

Condensed chromosome

Condensed chromatin

Extended chromatin

Coiled nucleosomes

Nucleosomes

DNA double helix

The DNA molecule in the nucleus is wrapped up in special covers called chromosomes. The total length of a DNA molecule wrapped up in the chromosomes is 1 metre. A chromosome is one nanometre thick, in other words a billionth of a metre. How is a 1-metre long DNA molecule contained in such a tiny space?

Chromosome packages are actually made up of much smaller special container systems. The DNA molecule is first wound around special proteins called histones, just like a cotton reel. Thus, they form structures called nucleosomes. These nucleosomes are specially designed to protect the DNA and stop it being damaged. When nucleosomes are strung on to one another, they form chromatins. Closely wound coiled loops form with the chromatin. In this way, a superb creation squeezes the DNA molecule into a tiny space only a billionth of its length.

Computers are currently the most advanced form of technology for storing information. A body of information, which, 30 years ago, was routinely stored in a computer the size of a room, can today be stored in small "discs," yet even the latest technology invented by human intelligence, after centuries of accumulated knowledge and years of hard work, is far from reaching the information storage capacity of a single cell nucleus. The following comparison made by the well-known professor of microbiology Michael Denton, will probably suffice to highlight the contrast between the tiny size of DNA and the great amount of information it contains:

> The information necessary to specify the design of all the species of organisms which have ever existed on the planet, a number according to G.G. Simpson of approximately one thousand million, could be held in a teaspoon and there would still be room left for all the information in every book ever written.[1]

How can a chain invisible to the eye, made up of atoms arranged sideways, with a diametre the size of a billionth of a millimetre, possess such information capacity and memory? And to this question also add the following: While each one of the 100 trillion cells in your body knows one million pages of information by heart, how many encyclopaedia pages can you, as an intelligent and conscious human being, memorize in your entire life? Even more important, the cell uses this information quite flawlessly, in an exceedingly planned and coordinated manner, in the appropriate places, and never makes any errors. Even before a human being has come into existence, his cells have already begun the process of building him.

Cells: Building Blocks of Humans

The fertilization of an egg by the sperm means the beginning of a new human life. Millions of sperm compete to fertilize the egg, although only one of them will manage to do so. Yet the race is not left to chance or coincidence, since every phase of it has been created by God with a fixed outcome. God reveals this truth in a holy verse:

We created you, so why do you not confirm the truth? Have you thought about the sperm that you ejaculate? Is it you who create it or are We the Creator? (Qur'an, 56:57-59)

When the father's sperm cell fertilizes the mother's egg cell, the parents' genes come together to determine all the physical characteristics of the baby that will eventually be born. Each of the thousands of different genes has a particular function. It is the genes that determine hair and eye colour, facial shape, and countless details in the skeleton, internal organs, brain, nerves and muscles.

When the sperm unites with the egg, a cell forms-the basis of a new human being-and along with that cell, the first copy of the DNA molecule also forms, which will carry that person's genetic code inside each cell all through his life.

In order for that first cell, the fertilized egg, to turn into a human being, it needs to multiply, and in the knowledge of that, it begins to divide, with a remarkable consciousness. That consciousness reveals itself in the next phase. As the cells divide, they begin to grow different and go to those parts of the body where they are needed. Instead of a mass of flesh composed of exactly the same cells, some of them turn into eye cells and go where they are needed, others form heart cells and go to the chest, and still others become skin cells

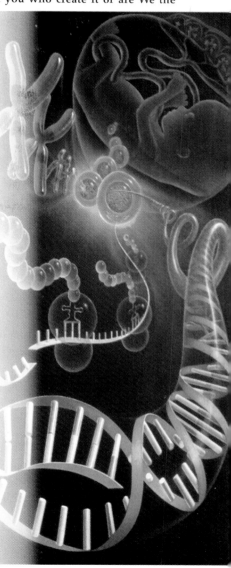

and cover the whole body. All the cells multiply as much as is needed for the particular tissue they will construct, and start joining together to give the tissues the structure they need, thus beginning to create different organs.

The coordination of this differentiation and structuring is made possible by the DNA molecule. We must not lose sight of the fact that DNA is neither a biochemist working in laboratories full of the very latest equipment, nor a super-computer able to perform trillions of calculations a second. DNA is a molecule made up of atoms such as carbon, phosphorous, nitrogen, hydrogen and oxygen.

Let us now consider the following facts: The trillions of cells in the human body multiply by dividing. Yet different genes in different cells are activated at different times, and that allows cells to differentiate. To put it another way, every cell that divides and multiplies after the first cell contains a complete set of genetic information. In other words, every single cell possesses the ability to produce heart muscle, skin, red blood cells or any other tissue in the body. Even though each cell contains a complete genetic description of the whole body, only some genes are active at different times in different organs. For instance, every cell contains the codes for the development and functioning of the kidneys, yet only the relevant genes are active in that organ, at certain times in the development phase. Similarly, certain enzymes, glucose-6-phospate for instance, are found mainly in the liver. Although all the cells of all other organs also possess the description of this protein, they never produce it. Eye cells never do; for example, they just make what is necessary for the eye: nerve cells will carry messages to and from the brain and the organs, liver cells will purify toxins, and fat cells store food for times when food is hard to find. None of them ever commit the error of producing stomach enzymes. So who carries out this flawless division of labor? Who orders the cells to specialise in different areas after they have divided and multiplied? Moreover, how do all the cells come by the consciousness to obey, and whom do they listen to while working with such flawless discipline and organization? It is quite clear that none of these are coincidental systems, formed as the result of yet other coincidences.

This flawlessness does not end with the fact that cells appear in the right place and at the right time, and bring the right genes into play. Cells also have to be present at the appropriate stage of life, and in the right quantities. Our "upkeep" genes work the whole time in almost all our cells. Other genes only function in some cells at a critical period in life, working for just a few hours before going into dormant mode. For instance, milk production is accelerated by genes during breastfeeding. Existing information is activated at the right time, in the right amount, at the right place. Evolutionists' use of "coincidence" to explain this conscious, planned, determined, calculated and intelligent direction and use of the billions of pieces of information concealed in DNA is really no explanation at all. No system in the world, not even the simplest, can come about by coincidence, so it is utterly illogical to see the extraordinarily planned and organised events that go on at the level of microscopic space as coincidences. In fact, evolutionists admit that they are far from offering an explanation for this differentiation and division of labour in cells. The evolutionist microbiologist Professor Ali Demirsoy makes this confession:

> In essence, no satisfactory explanation for the development of groups of cells with very different structures and functions has yet been provided.[2]

All these extraordinary events can clearly not be accounted for in terms of coincidences or being the work of the cells themselves. So, who directs these developments that occur in the cell, creates them for a particular purpose, and possesses the intelligence and power to introduce billions of pieces of information into a tiny space invisible to the naked eye?

The Wisdom in the Cell

In this case, you must admit that any cell in your stomach or ear is much more learned than you, and since it makes use of this information in the most correct and perfect way, it is much wiser than you.

But what is the source of this wisdom? How is it that every single one of the 100 trillion cells in the human body possesses such unbelievable intelligence, information and ability? These are, after all, piles of atoms, and they are unconscious. Take the atoms of all the elements, combine them in different forms and numbers, obtain different molecules, still you can never obtain wisdom. Whether these molecules are big or small, simple or complex does not matter. You can never obtain a mind that will consciously organise any process and accomplish it.

Then how can it be that DNA, which is composed of the arrangement of a certain number of unwise and unconscious atoms in certain sequences, and enzymes, working in a harmonious way, is able to organise countless complicated and diverse operations in the cell in a perfect and complete manner? The answer to this is very simple; wisdom is not in these molecules or in the cell that contains them, but in the self who has brought these molecules into being, programming them to function as they do. Shortly put, wisdom is present not in the work done, but in the creator of that work.

Even the most developed computer is the product of a wisdom and intellect that have written and installed the programs to operate it, and

If one day you see the words "Nothing comes about by chance" written on a piece of paper, you will not imagine they formed when ink was spilled on it. Every person of intelligence will think they were written by someone. Evolutionists' claims regarding the formation of the information inside DNA are just as totally illogical as saying that the letters on the piece of paper came about by chance.

11

then used it. Likewise, the cell, DNA and the RNAs in it, and the human being made up of these cells are nothing but the works of the One who created them as well as what they do. No matter how perfect, complete and striking the work is, the wisdom always lies with the owner of the work.

If you saw one meaningful sentence in your notebook on the table, you would be curious to know who wrote it. You would never think that the notebook and the pen or the ink came together with the effect of the wind and wrote this sentence. In DNA, we are talking about billions of pieces of information each of which is crucial for a human being.

So, why don't we ask the same question about the cell? If the information in the notebook or the computer was written by someone, then who "wrote" DNA, which has a far superior and more advanced technology, is designed in the most perfect manner, created, and placed in the tiny cell, which, by itself, is another miracle? Besides, to date it has not lost any of the properties which it has had for thousands of years. What can be more important for you than to question by whom and why these cells, that function non-stop so that you may read these lines, see, breathe, think, in brief, exist and continue to exist, have been brought into being?

Is not the answer to this question that which, in life, you must wonder about most? One sees great design, planning and order, from the sun in the sky to the DNA in one's body. To think that any of these things could be the work of chance is an unacceptable claim, one that is impossible to take seriously.

No Design Can Happen by Chance

You must have seen the name of a building spelt out in flowers on the ground in front of it. Looking down at them or from far away, you can immediately make out the name of the building or company concerned. That is a sign that the flowers are not there by chance, that they have been set out by gardeners and landscape designers. You may not see the gardeners actually doing it, but you can see that it has happened from the name the flowers spell out.

Alternatively, let us imagine that you leave the tiles scattered about at random on the table after a game of Scrabble. When you return, you see that the tiles now spell out the words: "I have won," and you immediately realize that someone has arranged them in a meaningful sequence. You would never imagine that they had come together by chance and formed those words, in just the same way that you would never imagine the name the flowers spelt out had appeared by chance. In short, if there is a design directed to a particular end somewhere, then you know that there must definitely be a designer behind it. You may not have seen the designer, yet you can be certain of his existence and intention from his work or the traces he leaves behind him.

The main idea we would like to convey with these examples is this: If there is even the slightest sign of something planned somewhere, there certainly lie the traces of a possessor of wisdom. For example, if you roll white stones down a mountain trillions of times, you will never see that they come to spell out the name of a building. If there is a word or a sentence somewhere, everyone will agree that that word or sentence must have been written by someone. Words without writers, or designs without designers are quite impossible.

Nobody will have any doubt that the parts of a watch in the picture were designed by somebody. The encoding of the information in DNA is even more magnificent than the design in a watch. That being the case, it is a great lie to claim that that information came about by chance as the result of a decision by unconscious atoms.

Think of a jigsaw like the one in the picture. Every single piece needs to be in its right place for the puzzle to be completed and a picture emerge. Just like a jigsaw, all the nucleotides need to be in the correct order set out for them in order for the DNA molecules to form a perfect living thing and allow it to survive.

It is of course ridiculous to think that the scattered pieces of a jigsaw puzzle came together by chance to make the picture below. It is even more illogical to claim that DNA, which has an incomparably more perfect design and complex coding system than a jigsaw puzzle, formed by coincidence.

The human body, on the other hand, possesses a structure trillions of times more complex than the name of a building or the words "I have won," and it is again totally impossible to imagine that this complexity could have come about of its own accord, or by chance. Moreover, the trillions of DNA that billions of living things have possessed for millions of years have been used in the most intelligent manner, written in the most perfect manner with no flaws, and placed in a tiny area invisible to the naked eye. That being the case, there is a Creator who planned and designed the cell and the DNA inside it so perfectly. Claiming the opposite means to go beyond the bounds of reason and attack the very foundations of truth, reason and logic.

Nevertheless, many people, who would readily say that it is impossible for letters to arrange themselves to form even three little words, can listen without objection to the deceit that it was all as a result of "coincidences" that billions of atoms came together one by one in a planned sequence and formed a molecule such as DNA, which performs such a super-complex task. This is just like a hypnotized person's submitting to the hypnotist and accepting by suggestion that he is a door, a tree or a lizard...

Flawless design samples in DNA are not limited to the above-mentioned examples. The coding of the data in DNA has been designed in a much more fascinating and amazing way.

The DNA Alphabet

The DNA in the cell nucleus has a spiral structure. When this is opened out, DNA turns into a long, thin string a metre or so in length. The way that a metre or so of DNA is squeezed into a minute cell nucleus is a subject requiring further consideration.

The atoms making up DNA have a superior design allowing the maximum amount of information to be carried in the smallest possible area. Three elements are found at every step of the two spiral ladders that twist around each other: sugar, phosphate and hydrogen-containing organic bases that make up the DNA codes. Although the tools and functions are the same in every human being, the particular codes that allow people to be different from one another are made up of these hydrogen bases. The differences in the way these four different bases are set out are the reason for all the differences between people. These bases are called Adenine, Guanine, Cytosine, and Thymine. They are linked to each other according to specific rules. Like a foreign language that scientists are just beginning to learn to read, these four types of hydrogen-based organic bases conceal the entire code of our biological existence.

These bases that make up the DNA molecule are known by their initial letters, A, T, G and C. The information in the data bank in the cell nucleus is stored in this way in an alphabet consisting of these four letters.

Each gene, which comprises one portion of the DNA molecule, determines a particular feature of the human body. Countless properties like height, eye colour, the material and the shape of the nose, ear, and skull are formed by the command of the related genes. We can compare every one of these genes to the pages of a book. On the pages there are scripts made up of the letters A – T – G – C.

There are approximately 200,000 genes in the DNA of a human cell. Every gene is composed of a special sequence of nucleotides, the number of which ranges between 1000 and 186,000 according to the type of the protein it correlates. These genes hold the codes of nearly 200,000 proteins that function in the human body and control the production of these proteins.

The Ordering of Genes

One of the most important discoveries of molecular biology was that some genes are more influential than others. The reason for this is that genes are set out in a very complicated order. In the fundamental genetic hierarchy there are genes charged with carrying out functions that are repeated: making haemoglobin, hair growth, or the production of digestive enzymes for instance. There are "ordering" genes placed over these worker molecules. These make the worker molecules work, and also stop them from doing so. For example, they stop the haemoglobin gene from functioning during childhood. There is a series of "main controls" over both the workers and "middle management." Their decisions affect dozens, even hundreds of sub-units. These genes are so vital that it can be fatal if they are damaged during the embryo stage.

That is a fact that requires careful consideration. Genes are molecules made up of atoms. So, how did these molecules set up such an ordered organization amongst themselves? How is it that a molecule can take the decision to halt someone's growth and relay that decision to other genes, so that they may receive, obey and implement it? Who set up that discipline? Furthermore, trillions of genes have been flawlessly carrying out the same functions for millions of years, with the same discipline, obedience, intelligence and consciousness.

To claim that such a system emerged by coincidence is utterly specious. There is no doubt that it is God, the Lord, who programs the genes so cleverly and perfectly.

DNA Challenges Coincidence

Today mathematics has proved that coincidence does not play a role in the formation of the coded information within DNA. Let alone the DNA molecule made up of millions of base pairs, the probability of the coincidental formation of even a single gene out of the 200,000 genes making up DNA is so low that even the word "impossible" hardly expresses it. Frank Salisbury, an evolutionist biologist, makes the following statement about this "impossibility:"

> A medium protein might include about 300 amino acids. The DNA gene controlling this would have about 1,000 nucleotides in its chain. Since there

are four kinds of nucleotides in a DNA chain, one consisting of 1,000 links could exist in 4^{1000} forms. Using a little algebra (logarithms) we can see that $4^{1000}=10^{600}$. Ten multiplied by itself 600 times gives the figure 1 followed by 600 zeros! This number is completely beyond our comprehension.[3]

That is to say that even if we assume that all the necessary nucleotides are present in a medium, and that all the complex molecules and enzymes to combine them were available, the possibility of these nucleotides being arranged in the desired sequence is 1 in 4^{1000}, in other words, 1 in 10^{600}. Briefly, the probability of the coincidental formation of the code of an average protein in the human body in DNA by itself is 1 over 1 followed by 600 zeros. This number, which is beyond even being astronomical, means in practice "zero" probability. This means that such a sequence has to be effected under the control and with the knowledge of a wise and conscious power. There is zero probability of it happening by "accident," "chance," or "coincidence."

Francis Crick and James Watson won the Nobel Prize for discovering the magnificent structure of DNA.

Think of the book you are reading right now. How would you regard someone who claimed that letters have come together by chance on their own to form this writing? It is evident that it was written by an intelligent and conscious person. This is no different from the status of DNA.

Francis Crick, the biochemist who discovered the structure of DNA, won a Nobel prize for the research he had carried out on the subject. Crick, who was an ardent evolutionist, stated the

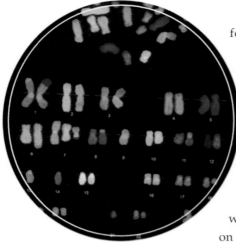

Human cells contain 46 chromosomes, in 23 pairs. Each pair is responsible for certain activities in the body. Any defect in the chromosome pairs results in irreparable damage.

following scientific opinion in a book he wrote after testifying to the miraculous structure of DNA: "An honest man, armed with all the knowledge available to us now, could only state that, in some sense, the origin of life appears at the moment to be almost a miracle."[4] Even in Crick's view, who was one of the biggest experts on DNA, life could never originate on earth spontaneously.

When we consider the sensitive order and balances in the data inside DNA, it becomes even clearer how it is impossible for them to have come about by chance. The data in DNA, which is made up of 3 billion letters, is composed of a special and meaningful sequence of the letters A-T-G-C. However, not even a single letter should be misplaced in this sequence. A misspelled word or a single letter error in an encyclopaedia may be overlooked and ignored. It would not even be noticed. However, even a single mistake in any base pair of DNA, such as a miscoded letter in the 1 billion 719 million 348 thousand 632nd base pair, would cause terrible results for the cell, and therefore for the person himself. For instance, haemophilia (leukaemia) is the outcome of such an erroneous coding. There are several hereditary diseases that are caused by various disorders in genetic make-up. The only reason for these potentially very threatening diseases is that one or a few of the millions of letters in the genetic code are in the wrong place. Mongolism, or Down's Syndrome, is quite widespread. It is caused by the presence of an extra chromosome in the 21st chromosome pair in every cell. Another example is Huntington's Disease. The sufferer is quite healthy up to 35, but then uncontrollable muscular spasms appear in the arms, legs and face. Since this fatal and incurable disease also affects the brain, the sufferer's memory and powers of thought grow progressively weaker.

All these genetic diseases reveal one important fact: the genetic code is so sensitive and balanced, and so minutely calculated, that the smallest change can lead to very serious consequences. One letter too many or too few can lead to fatal sicknesses, or lifelong crippling effects. For this reason, it is definitely impossible to think that such a sensitive equilibrium

A Downs Syndrome child with one extra chromosome in the 21st chromosome pair.

came about by chance and developed by means of mutations, as the theory of evolution would have us believe. That being the case, how did the enormous information within DNA come about and how was it encoded? Evolutionists, who base the roots of life on coincidences, have actually no comment to make on the subject of the roots of life. When you ask them about the roots of DNA, in other words the genetic code, you get the same reply from all of them. Leslie E. Orgel for instance, one of the foremost evolutionist biochemists of our time, offers the following reply:

> We do not understand even the general features of the origin of the genetic code . . . [It] is the most baffling aspect of the problem of the origins of life and a major conceptual or experimental breakthrough may be needed before we can make any substantial progress.[5]

Those who claim that millions of pages, billions of pieces of information were written by chance are of course left quite speechless in this way. In the same way that every book or piece of information has a writer or owner, so does the information in DNA: and that Creator is our Lord God, the possessor of superior and infinite knowledge and reason.

A Unique Creation: Self-Replication of DNA

As we know, cells multiply by dividing. While the human body is initially composed of a single cell, this cell divides and reproduces itself many times over in a ratio of 2-4-8-16-32...

What happens to DNA at the end of this dividing process? There is only one DNA chain in the cell. However, it is evident that the newly formed cell will also require a DNA. In order to fill this gap, DNA completes an interesting series of operations, every phase of which is a different miracle. Finally, soon before the cell divides, it makes a copy of itself and transfers this to the new cell.

Observations of cell division show that the cell has to reach a specific size before dividing. The moment it exceeds this particular size, the division process automatically starts. While the shape of the cell begins to get smoother so as to accommodate the division process, DNA starts to replicate itself as mentioned earlier.

This means that the cell "decides" to divide as a whole and the different parts of the cell start to act in accordance with this decision. It is evident that the cell is devoid of the consciousness to accomplish such a collective action. The division process starts with a secret order and the entire cell, including DNA, acts on this order.

First, DNA divides into two to replicate itself. This event takes place in a very interesting manner. The DNA molecule which resembles a spiral ladder divides into two like a zip from the middle of the rungs of the ladder. From now on, DNA divides into two portions. The missing halves (replicates) of both of the two portions are completed with the materials present in the milieu. In this way, two new DNA molecules

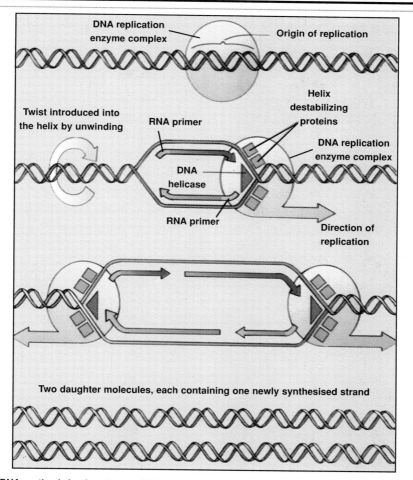

DNA replication enzyme complex

Origin of replication

Twist introduced into the helix by unwinding

RNA primer

Helix destabilizing proteins

DNA replication enzyme complex

DNA helicase

RNA primer

Direction of replication

Two daughter molecules, each containing one newly synthesised strand

DNA synthesis begins at a specific base sequence, known as the origin of replication. Here, DNA strands are separated by an enzyme known as DNA helicase, following which single stranded DNA binding proteins attach to the unwound strands, preventing them from winding back together. At the same time, an RNA molecule known as RNA primer is synthesised between the strands as they detach themselves. This molecule helps DNA polymerase read nucleotides and initiate replication. DNA polymerase binds to one strand of the DNA, reads the sequence of bases on the template strand and then synthesises the complementary strand. Thus, it reforms a double helix. DNA synthesis proceeds on both single strands in opposite directions. When the process comes to an end, two new daughter molecules emerge, each containing one newly synthesised strand.

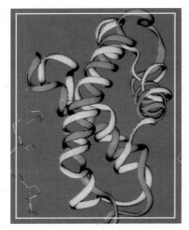

Thanks to the information within DNA, the proteins that undertake countless tasks in our bodies are produced with all the features they need.

are produced. In every phase of the operation, expert proteins called "enzymes" that function like advanced robots take part. Though it seems simple at first sight, the intermediary processes taking place throughout this operation are so many and so complicated that to describe the whole event in detail would take pages.

One thing must not be forgotten here. The enzymes that form as a result of atoms coming together examine one half of the DNA spiral, identify those parts that are missing, take the missing parts from the appropriate places and add them where needed. In this way, the copying of DNA comes about. The way that tiny unconscious, unreasoning structures can flawlessly carry out such complex processes, that require consciousness, knowledge and reason is not to be glossed over by just reading about them. There are important truths revealed here that need to be considered.

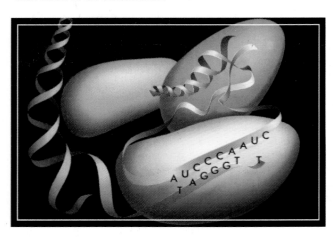

A special enzyme, called telomerase directs the replication of telomeres. Telomere is the end of a chromosome, which consists of repeated sequences of DNA that perform the function of ensuring that each cycle of DNA replication has been completed.

strand

strand

} base pairs

sugar-phosphate
backbone

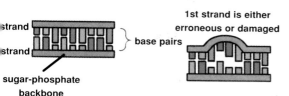

**1st strand is either
erroneous or damaged**

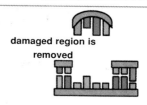

**damaged region is
removed**

**DNA polymerase enzyme
identifies and inserts the
correct nucleotide.**

**Once the correct
nucleotide is incorporated,
the resulting nicks in the
DNA are sealed by a DNA
ligase. Now the 1st strand
is repaired.**

DNA repairs itself and permits no errors.
When the DNA synthesis is complete, an error occurs in one nucleotide in a thousand. Yet
such errors have been prepared for. There is a special group of enzymes charged with
repairing errors that occur during the DNA synthesis. These enzymes identify the error in a
conscious manner and remove the defective nucleotide. They synthetise a new nucleotide
and insert it back during the process.

The new DNA molecules that emerge during replication are checked
repeatedly by inspector enzymes. If any mistake is made-which can be
quite vital, it is immediately identified and corrected. The erroneous code
is removed and replaced by the correct one. Although all these processes
take place at such a dazzling speed-3,000 base pairs are produced in a
minute,-all these pairs are checked repeatedly by the enzymes in charge
and the necessary amendments are made.

The following facts, which are particularly revealing will give a
better understanding of the great speed at which DNA multiplies. The
division of one cell lasts between 20 and 80 minutes, and the information
on DNA needs to be copied and multiplied within that time scale. In other
words, the 3 billion pieces of information in DNA can be copied in
between 20 and 80 minutes with no faults or omissions. That is as
miraculous as the perfect reproduction in such a short space of time as all
the information in a library, or 1,000 books, or a million pages. And note
carefully, it is not technological equipment or advanced photocopiers that
do this, but enzymes formed by collections of atoms.

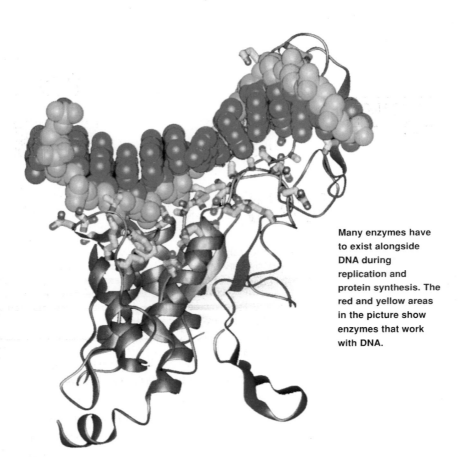

Many enzymes have to exist alongside DNA during replication and protein synthesis. The red and yellow areas in the picture show enzymes that work with DNA.

In the newly produced DNA molecule, more mistakes can be made than normal as a result of external factors. In this case, the ribosomes in the cell start to produce DNA repair enzymes as per the order given by DNA. Thus, as DNA protects itself, it also guarantees the preservation of the generation.

The cells are born, they reproduce and die just like human beings. Yet the life spans of cells are much shorter than the life of the human they constitute. For instance, the majority of the cells that used to make up your body six months ago do not exist today. However, you are now able to survive because they have divided on time to leave their places to the new ones. For this reason, highly complex operations like multiplication of the cells and replication of DNA are vital processes which cannot tolerate even a minor mistake when it comes to man's survival. However, the multiplication process runs so smoothly that the rate of error is only one in 3 billion base pairs. And this one error is eliminated by the higher control mechanisms in the body without causing any problems.

The most interesting point is that these enzymes which help in the production of DNA and control its composition are actually proteins produced according to the information coded in DNA and under the command and control of DNA. There is such an intertwined, perfect system at work that it is by no means possible for such a system to have attained this state by gradual coincidences. Just as DNA has to exist for the enzyme to exist, so the enzyme has to exist for DNA to exist, and for both to exist, on the other hand, the cell has to exist completely, down to its membrane and all the other complex organelles it contains.

The theory of evolution asserting that living beings evolved "step by step" as a result of "beneficial coincidences" is explicitly refuted by the above mentioned DNA-enzyme paradox. This is because both DNA and the enzyme have to exist at the same time. And this shows the existence of a conscious creation.

All through the day, quite without your being aware of it, numerous operations and controls are carried out, and many measures are taken in your body in an incredibly fastidious and responsible manner so that you may lead your life without any problems. Every single thing carries out its duty successfully and completely. God has placed at your service countless atoms and molecules, from the biggest to the smallest, from the simplest to the most complex, so that you may live a good and healthy life. Such favour and blessing alone are enough to deserve our constant thanks.

It was God who made the night for you to rest in, and the day to give you light. God pours out His favour on mankind, yet most people do not give thanks. (Qur'an, 40:61)

DARWINISM CANNOT EXPLAIN
HOW THE INFORMATION IN DNA ORIGINATED
AND HOW IT DIFFERS IN EVERY SPECIES

Evolutionists can in no way offer any explanation on the subject of how DNA originated, and there is yet another point where they reach an impasse. How is it that fish, reptiles, insects, birds or human beings came to have different DNA, different genetic information?

Evolutionists answer that question by saying that the body of information in DNA developed and diversified over time by means of coincidences. The coincidences they refer to are "mutations." Mutations are changes which take place in DNA as a result of radiation or chemical action. Sometimes radioactive radiation happens to fall on a DNA chain and destroys or displaces several base pairs therein. According to evolutionists, living things have reached their present perfect state as a result of the diversification of a single DNA due to these mutations (i.e., accidents).

To show that this claim is unreasonable, let us again compare DNA to a book. We have already mentioned that DNA is made up of letters lined up sideways just as in a book. Mutations are like the letter errors that occur during the type-setting of this book. If you like, we can do an experiment on this subject. Let us ask for a thick book about the history of the world to be type-set. During the type-setting, let us intervene several times and tell the type-setter to press one of the keys blindfolded and at random. Then let us give this text containing letter errors to someone else and have him do the same thing over again. Using this method, let us have the book type-set from the beginning to the end several times, thus having a few more letter errors added to it at random each time...

Could this history book ever develop by this method? For instance, would an additional chapter emerge, named, "The History of Ancient China," when it had previously not been present?

To be sure, the letter errors we have added to the book would not develop it, but rather ruin it and distort its meaning. The more we increase the number of faulty copying processes, the more spoiled our book will be.

Yet the claim of the theory of evolution is that "letter errors help develop a book." According to evolution, mutations (errors) occurring in DNA have led to beneficial results by accumulating and thus furnishing living beings with perfect organs such as eyes, ears, wings, hands and consciousness-related qualities such as thinking, learning, and reasoning.

Unquestionably, this claim is even more unreasonable than the above example of the addition of the chapter called "The History of Ancient China" to a book on world history as a result of the accumulation of letter errors. (Moreover there is no mechanism in nature that causes regular mutations as in the example of the type-setter making regular mistakes. The mutations in nature take place much more rarely than the letter errors that would occur during the type-setting of a book.)

Every "explanation" put forward by the theory of evolution on the origin of life is unreasonable and unscientific. One outspoken authority on this issue is the famous French zoologist Pierre Grassé, the former president of the French Academy of Sciences. Grassé is also an evolutionist, but he states clearly that Darwinist theory is unable to explain life and makes his point about the logic of "coincidence," which is the backbone of Darwinism:

> The opportune appearance of mutations permitting animals and plants to meet their needs seems hard to believe. Yet the Darwinian theory is even more demanding: A single plant, a single animal would require thousands and thousands of lucky, appropriate events. Thus, miracles would become the rule: events with an infinitesimal probability could not fail to occur... There is no law against day-dreaming, but science must not indulge in it.[6]

Indeed, the theory of evolution, which claims that lifeless matter came together by itself and formed living beings with such glorious systems as DNA, is a scenario totally contrary to science and reason. All this leads us to an evident conclusion. Since life has a plan (DNA) and all living beings are fashioned according to this plan, it is evident that there is a superior Creator who devised this plan. This simply means that all living beings are created by God, the All-Powerful, All-Wise. God states this fact in the Qur'an in this way:

He is God – the Creator, the Maker, the Giver of Form. To Him belong the Most Beautiful Names. Everything in the heavens and earth glorifies Him. He is the Almighty, the All-Wise. (Qur'an, 59:24)

Today, what people have achieved by means of technology can at best be described as "an approach to the understanding of a tiny fragment of God's knowledge, as manifested in human DNA."

DNA CONFESSIONS
FROM EVOLUTIONISTS

The question of how such an extraordinarily designed molecule as DNA originated is one of the thousands of impasses evolutionists reach. Seeking to explain life by means of "coincidence," the theory of evolution can never explain the source of the extraordinary information so perfectly and meticulously encoded in DNA.

Moreover, the question is not only that of how the DNA chain originated. That is because, as we have already seen, although the DNA chain exists with its extraordinary information capacity, it serves no purpose on its own. In order to refer to life, it is essential that the enzymes that read this DNA chain, copy them and produce proteins, should also exist.

Simply put, in order to talk of life, both the data bank we call DNA, and the machines to carry out production by reading the data in the bank have to co-exist.

To our surprise, enzymes, which read DNA and carry out production accordingly, are themselves produced according to the codes in DNA. This means that there is a factory in the cell that both makes many different types of products, and also manufactures the robots and machines that carry out this production. The question of how this system, which would be of no use with a minor defect in any of its mechanisms originated, is by itself enough to demolish the theory of evolution.

Evolutionist Douglas R. Hofstadter of Indiana University, states his despair in the face of this question:

"How did the Genetic Code, along with the mechanisms for its translation (ribosomes and RNA molecules), originate?" For the moment, we will have to content ourselves with a sense of wonder and awe, rather than with an answer.[7]

Another evolutionist authority, world renowned molecular biologist Leslie Orgel, is more outspoken on the subject:

It is extremely improbable that proteins and nucleic acids, both of which are structurally complex, arose spontaneously in the same place at the same time. Yet it also seems impossible to have one without the other. And so, at first glance, ONE MIGHT HAVE TO CONCLUDE THAT LIFE COULD NEVER, IN FACT, HAVE ORIGINATED BY CHEMICAL MEANS.[8]

Saying "life could never have originated by chemical means" is the equivalent of saying that "life could never have originated by itself." Recognition of the truth of this statement results in the realization that life is created in a conscious way. For ideological reasons, evolutionists, however, do not accept this fact, clear evidence of which is before their eyes. To avoid accepting the existence of God, they believe in nonsensical scenarios, despite their evident impossibility.

Another evolutionist, Caryl P. Haskins, states how the DNA code could not have emerged by chance, and that this fact is strong evidence for creation:

But the most sweeping evolutionary questions at the level of biochemical genetics are still unanswered. How the genetic code first appeared and then evolved and, earlier even than that, how life itself originated on earth remain for the future to resolve.... Did the code and the means of translating it appear simultaneously in evolution? It seems almost incredible that any such coincidence could have occurred, given the extraordinary complexities of both sides and the requirement that they be coordinated accurately for survival. By a pre-Darwinian (or a skeptic of evolution after Darwin) this

puzzle would surely have been interpreted as the most powerful sort of evidence for special creation.[9]

In his book *Evolution: A Theory in Crisis*, writing of the invalidity of the theory of evolution, renowned molecular biologist Prof. Michael Denton explains the unreasonable conviction of Darwinists:

To the skeptic, the proposition that the genetic programmes of higher organisms, consisting of something close to a thousand million bits of information, equivalent to the sequence of letters in a small library of one thousand volumes, containing in encoded form countless thousands of intricate algorithms controlling, specifying, and ordering the growth and development of billions and billions of cells into the form of a complex organism, were composed by a purely random process is simply AN AFFRONT TO REASON. BUT TO THE DARWINIST, THE IDEA IS ACCEPTED WITHOUT A RIPPLE OF DOUBT - THE PARADIGM TAKES PRECEDENCE![10]

Prof. Michael Denton

Indeed, Darwinism is nothing but a totally unreasonable, superstitious belief. Anyone with any reason would see the evidence for that great fact by looking at DNA, or any other part of the universe. Human beings and all living things are created by God, the Almighty, who is the Lord of all the worlds.

Another example of evolutionists' helplessness: The "RNA World" Scenario

Ever since the start of the 20th century, evolutionists have developed various theories to explain how the first living cell emerged. The Russian biologist Alexander Oparin, who proposed the first evolutionary thesis on the subject, suggested that in the primitive world of hundreds of millions of years ago, a series of coincidental chemical reactions led to first of all proteins, and that cells were then born when these came together. Discoveries made in the 1970s showed that even the most fundamental assumptions of this claim, which Oparin made in the 1930s, were mistaken. Oparin's "primitive world atmosphere" scenario contained the gases methane and ammonia to allow the formation of organic molecules. However, it was realized that the hypothesis of an early methane-ammonia atmosphere is without solid foundation and indeed is contradicted, and that the early atmophere contained a large amount of oxygen which destroys organic molecules as they form.

This was a big blow to the theory of molecular evolution. Evolutionists then had to face the fact that the "primitive atmosphere experiments" by Stanley Miller, Sidney Fox and Cyril Ponnamperuma and others were invalid. For this reason, in the 1980s evolutionists tried again. As a result, "RNA World" hypothesis was advanced. This scenario proposed that, not proteins, but rather the RNA molecules that contained the information for proteins were formed first. According to this scenario advanced by Harvard chemist Walter Gilbert in 1986, billions of years ago

an RNA molecule capable of replicating itself, formed somehow by accident. Then this RNA molecule started to produce proteins, having

When the Urey-Miller experiment was invalidated, evolutionists had to embark on a new search.

been activated by external influences. Thereafter, it became necessary to store this information in a second molecule, and somehow the DNA molecule emerged to do that.

Made up of a chain of impossibilities in each and every stage, this scarcely credible scenario, far from providing any explanation of the origin of life, only magnified the problem and raised many unanswerable questions:

1. Since it is impossible to explain the coincidental formation of even one of the nucleotides making up RNA, how can it be possible for these imaginary nucleotides to form RNA by coming together in a particular sequence? Evolutionist John Horgan admits the impossibility of the chance formation of RNA:

> **As researchers continue to examine the RNA-world concept closely, more problems emerge**. How did RNA initially arise? RNA and its components are difficult to synthesize in a laboratory under the best of conditions, much less under really plausible ones.[11]

2. Even if we suppose that it formed by chance, how could this RNA consisting of just a nucleotide chain have "decided" to self-replicate and with what kind of a mechanism could it have carried out this self-replicating process? Where did it find the nucleotides it used while self-replicating? Even evolutionist microbiologists Gerald Joyce and Leslie Orgel express the desperateness of the situation in their book titled *In the RNA World:*

> This discussion... has, in a sense, **focused on a straw man: the myth of a self-replicating RNA molecule** that arose de novo from a soup of random polynucleotides. Not only is such a notion unrealistic in light of our current understanding of prebiotic chemistry, but it would **strain the credulity of even an optimist's view of RNA's catalytic potential**.[12]

3. Even if we suppose that there was self-replicating RNA in the primordial world, that numerous amino acids of every type ready to be used by RNA were available and that all of these impossibilities somehow took place, the situation still does not lead to the formation of even one single protein. For RNA only includes information concerning the

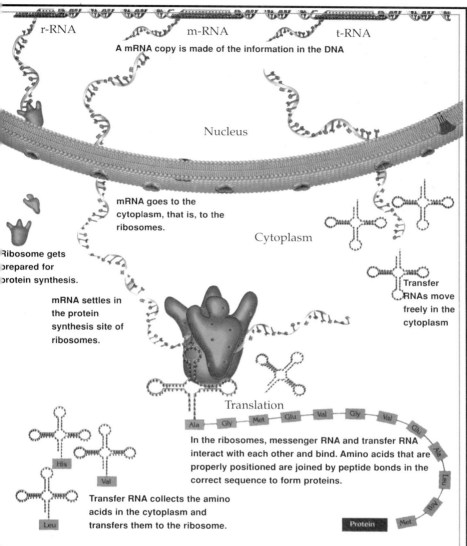

r-RNA   m-RNA   t-RNA

A mRNA copy is made of the information in the DNA

Nucleus

mRNA goes to the cytoplasm, that is, to the ribosomes.

Cytoplasm

Ribosome gets prepared for protein synthesis.

mRNA settles in the protein synthesis site of ribosomes.

Transfer RNAs move freely in the cytoplasm

Translation

Ala — Gly — Met — Glu — Val — Gly — Val — Glu — Ala — Leu — Asp — Met — Protein

In the ribosomes, messenger RNA and transfer RNA interact with each other and bind. Amino acids that are properly positioned are joined by peptide bonds in the correct sequence to form proteins.

His

Val

Leu

Transfer RNA collects the amino acids in the cytoplasm and transfers them to the ribosome.

When the need is felt for a protein in a cell, a signal is sent to the DNA molecule. The DNA molecule receiving the signal understands which protein is needed. Then the DNA makes an RNA copy carrying specific information for making a protein, which is called messenger RNA. After receiving the information, mRNA leaves the nucleus and heads straight for the ribosomes, the protein production factory. At the same time, another RNA copied from the DNA, called transfer RNA, carries the amino acids for the proteins to the ribosomes. Each tRNA is an "adapter" molecule that can link with a specific amino acid. The tRNA which carries the amino acid sequence information of the protein to be formed settles in the production site of the ribosome. The amino acids brought by the tRNA take their places according to the sequence notified by the messenger RNA. Then another RNA molecule copied from DNA, called ribosomal RNA, enables the messenger and transfer RNAs to join together. Amino acids brought in by the transfer RNAs develop peptide bonds to form protein chains. The messenger RNAs leave the ribosome having deposited their loads. The protein that is produced then proceeds to where it will be used.

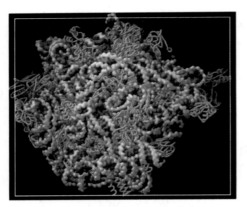

The above picture shows protein chains produced in the ribosome.

structure of proteins. Amino acids, on the other hand, are raw materials. Nevertheless, there is no mechanism for the production of proteins. To consider the existence of RNA sufficient for protein production is as nonsensical as expecting a car to assemble itself by simply throwing the blueprint onto a heap of parts piled on top of each other. A blueprint cannot produce a car all by itself without a factory and workers to assemble the parts according to the instructions contained in the blueprint; in the same way, the blueprint contained in RNA cannot produce proteins by itself without the cooperation of other cellular components which follow the instructions in the RNA.

Proteins are produced in the ribosome factory with the help of many enzymes, and as a result of extremely complex processes within the cell. The ribosome is a complex cell organelle made up of proteins. This leads, therefore, to another unreasonable supposition-that ribosomes, too, should have come into existence by chance at the same time. Even Nobel Prize winner Jacques Monod, who was one of the most fanatical defenders of evolution, explained that protein synthesis can by no means be considered to depend merely on the information in the nucleic acids:

> The code is meaningless unless translated. The modern cell's translating machinery consists of at least 50 macromolecular components, which are themselves coded in DNA: **the code cannot be translated otherwise than by products of translation themselves**. It is the modern expression of *omne vivum ex ovo* [all life from eggs, or idiomatically, what came first, the chicken or the egg?]. When and how did this circle become closed? **It is exceedingly difficult to imagine**.[13]

How could an RNA chain in the primordial world have taken such a decision, and what methods could it have employed to make protein production happen by doing the work of 50 macromolecular components on its own? Evolutionists have no answer to these questions.

Dr. Leslie Orgel, one of the associates of Stanley Miller and Francis Crick from the University of California at San Diego, uses the term "scenario" for the possibility of "the

Dr. Leslie Orgel

origination of life through the RNA world." Orgel described what kind of features this RNA would have had to have and how impossible these would have been in his article, "The Origin of Life," published in *American Scientist* in October 1994:

> This **scenario** could have occurred, we noted, if prebiotic RNA had two properties **not evident today**: A capacity **to replicate without the help of proteins and an ability to catalyze every step of protein synthesis.**[14]

As should by now be clear, to expect these two complex and extremely essential processes from a molecule such as RNA is only possible from the evolutionist's viewpoint and with the help of his power of imagination. Concrete scientific facts, on the other hand, make it explicit that the "RNA World" hypothesis, which is a new model proposed for the chance formation of life, is an equally implausible fable.

Life Cannot Be Explained by the Coming Together of Lifeless Molecules

Let us forget all the impossibilities for a moment and suppose that a protein molecule was formed in the most inappropriate, most uncontrolled environment such as the primordial earth conditions.

The formation of only one protein would not be sufficient; this protein would have to wait patiently in this uncontrolled environment

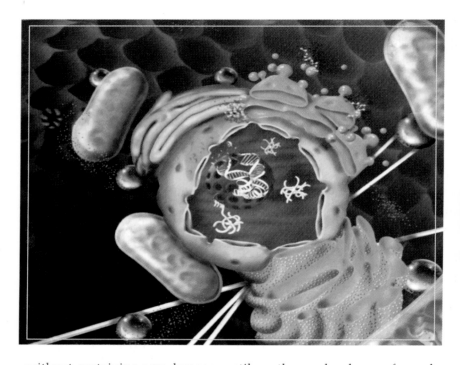

without sustaining any damage, until another molecule was formed beside it by chance under the same conditions. It would have to wait until millions of correct and essential proteins were formed side by side in the same setting all "by chance." Those that formed earlier had to be patient enough to wait, without being destroyed despite ultraviolet rays and harsh mechanical effects, for the others to be formed right next to them. Then these proteins in adequate number, which all originated at the very same spot, would have to come together by making meaningful combinations and form the organelles of the cell. No extraneous material, harmful molecule, or useless protein chain would have to interfere with them. Then, even if these organelles were to come together in an extremely harmonious and co-operative way with a plan and order, they should have to bring all the necessary enzymes close to themselves and become covered with a membrane, the inside of which would have to be filled with a special liquid to prepare the ideal environment for them.

Now even if all these "highly unlikely" events actually occurred by chance, would this molecular heap come to life?

The answer is "No," because research has revealed that the **mere combination of all the materials essential for life is not enough for life to get started.** Even if all the essential proteins for life were collected and put in a test tube, these efforts would not result in producing a living cell. All the experiments conducted on this subject have proved to be unsuccessful. All

Prof. Chandra Wickramasinghe

observations and experiments indicate that life can originate only from life. The assertion that life evolved from non-living things, in other words, "abiogenesis," is a tale existing only in the dreams of the evolutionists and completely at variance with the results of every experiment and observation.

In this respect, the first life on earth must also have originated from other life. This is a reflection of God's epithet of "Hayy" (The Alive, The Ever-Living). Life can only start, continue, and end by His will. As for evolution, not only is it unable to explain how life began, it is also unable to explain how the materials essential for life have formed and come together.

Chandra Wickramasinghe of Cardiff University describes the reality he faced as a scientist who had been told throughout his life that life had emerged as a result of chance coincidences:

> From my earliest training as a scientist, I was very strongly brainwashed to believe that science cannot be consistent with any kind of deliberate creation. That notion has had to be painfully shed. At the moment, I can't find any rational argument to knock down the view which argues for conversion to God. We used to have an open mind; now **we realize that the only logical answer to life is creation**-and not accidental random shuffling.[15]

THE SECOND LAW OF THERMODYNAMI

The second law of thermo-dynamics, which is accepted as one of the basic laws of physics, holds that under normal conditions all systems left on their own will tend to become disordered, dispersed, and corrupted in direct relation to the amount of time that passes. Everything, whether living or not, wears out, deteriorates, decays, disintegrates, and is destroyed. This is the absolute end that all beings will face one way or another, and according to the law, the process cannot be avoided.

This is something that all of us have observed. For example if you take a car to a desert and leave it there, you would hardly expect to find it in a better condition when you came back years later. On the contrary, you would see that its tyres had gone flat, its windows had been broken, its chassis had rusted, and its engine had stopped working. The same inevitable process holds true for living things.

The second law of thermodynamics is the means by which this natural process is defined, with physical equations and calculations.

This famous law of physics is also known as "the law of entropy." In physics, entropy is the measure of the disorder of a system. A system's entropy increases as it moves towards from an ordered, organised, and planned state towards a more disordered, dispersed, and unplanned one. The more disorder there is in a system, the higher its entropy is. The law of entropy holds that the entire universe is unavoidably proceeding towards a more disordered, unplanned, and disorganised state.

The truth of the second law of thermodynamics, or the entropy law, has been experimentally and theoretically established. All foremost scientists agree that the law of entropy will remain the principle paradigm for the foreseeable future. Albert Einstein, the greatest scientist of our age, described it as the "premier law of all science." Sir Arthur Eddington also referred to it as the "supreme metaphysical law of the entire universe."[1]

Evolutionary theory ignores this fundamental law of physics. The mechanism offered by evolution totally contradicts the second law. The theory of evolution says that disordered, dispersed, and lifeless atoms and molecules spontaneously came together over time, in a particular order, to form extremely complex molecules such as proteins, DNA, and RNA, whereupon millions of different living species with even more complex structures gradually emerged. According to the theory of evolution, this supposed process-which yields a more planned, more ordered, more complex and more organised structure at each stage-was formed all by itself under natural conditions. The law of entropy makes it clear that this so-called natural process utterly contradicts the laws of physics.

Evolutionist scientists are also aware of this fact. J.H. Rush states:

In the complex course of its evolution, life exhibits a remarkable contrast to the

If you leave a bus unattended in the desert it will gradually fall apart and lose all its features. The next time you look, you see the tyres have burst, the windows have broken, the bodywork is rusted and the engine has failed. This inevitable process happens even faster in living things. In the same manner, all systems in the universe fall apart without conscious intervention.

tendency expressed in the Second Law of Thermodynamics. Where the Second Law expresses an irreversible progression toward increased entropy and disorder, life evolves continually higher levels of order.[2]

The evolutionist author Roger Lewin expresses the thermodynamic impasse of evolution in an article in *Science*:

One problem biologists have faced is the apparent contradiction by evolution of the second law of thermodynamics. Systems should decay through time, giving less, not more, order.[3]

Another defender of the theory of evolution, George Stravropoulos, states the thermodynamic impossibility of the spontaneous formation of life and the impossibility of explaining the existence of complex living mechanisms by natural laws in the well-known evolutionist journal *American Scientist*:

Yet, under ordinary conditions, no complex organic molecule can ever form spontaneously, but will rather disintegrate, in agreement with the second law. Indeed, the more complex it is, the more unstable it will be, and the more assured, sooner or later, its disintegration. Photosynthesis and all life processes, and even life itself, *cannot* yet be understood in terms of thermodynamics or any other exact science, despite the use of confused or deliberately confusing language.[4]

As we have seen, the second law of thermodynamics constitutes an insurmountable obstacle for the scenario of evolution, in terms of both science and logic. Unable to offer any scientific and consistent explanation to overcome this obstacle, evolutionists can only do so in their imagination. For instance, the well-known evolutionist Jeremy Rifkin notes his belief that evolution overwhelms this law of physics with a "magical power:"

The Entropy Law says that evolution

dissipates the overall available energy for life on this planet. Our concept of evolution is the exact opposite. We believe that evolution somehow magically creates greater overall value and order on earth.[5]

These words well indicate that evolution is a dogmatic belief rather than a scientific thesis.

The Myth of the "Open System"

Confronted by all these truths, evolutionists have had to take refuge in a mangling of the second law of thermodynamics, saying that it holds true only for "closed systems," and that "open systems" are beyond the scope of this law.

An "open system" is a thermodynamic system in which energy and matter flow in and out. Evolutionists hold that the world is an open system: that it is constantly exposed to an energy flow from the sun, that the law of entropy does not apply to the world as a whole, and that ordered, complex living beings can be generated from disordered, simple, and inanimate structures.

However, there is an obvious distortion here. The fact that a system has an energy inflow is not enough to make that system ordered. Specific mechanisms are needed to make the energy functional. For instance, a car needs an engine, a transmission system, and related control mechanisms to convert the energy in petrol to work. Without such an energy conversion system, the car will not be able to use the energy in petrol.

The same thing applies in the case of life as well. It is true that life derives its energy from the sun. However, solar energy can only be converted into chemical energy by the incredibly complex energy conversion systems in living things (such as photosynthesis in plants and the digestive systems of humans and animals). No living thing can live without such energy conversion systems. Without an energy conversion system, the sun is nothing but a source of destructive energy that burns, parches, or melts.

As can be seen, a thermodynamic system without an energy conversion mechanism of some sort is not advantageous for evolution, be it open or closed. No one asserts that such complex and conscious mechanisms could have existed in nature under the conditions of the primeval earth. Indeed, the real problem confronting evolutionists is the question of how complex energy-converting mechanisms, such as photosynthesis in plants, which cannot be duplicated even with modern technology, could have come into being on their own.

The influx of solar energy into the world would be unable to bring about order on its own. Moreover, no matter how high the temperature may become, amino acids resist forming bonds in ordered sequences. Energy by itself is incapable of making amino acids form the much more complex molecules of proteins, or of making proteins form the much more complex and organised structures of cell organelles. The real and essential source of this organisation at all levels is conscious design: in a word, creation.

The "Chaos Theory" Evasion

Quite aware that the second law of thermodynamics renders evolution impossible, some evolutionist scientists have made speculative attempts to square the circle between the two, in order to be able to claim that evolution is possible. As usual, even those endeavours show that the theory of evolution faces an inescapable impasse.

One person distinguished by his efforts to marry thermodynamics and evolution is the Belgian scientist Ilya Prigogine.

Starting out from chaos theory, Prigogine proposed a number of hypotheses in which order forms from chaos (disorder). However, despite all his best efforts, he was unable to reconcile thermodynamics and evolution. This is clearly seen in what he says:

There is another question, which has plagued us for more than a century: What significance does the evolution of a living being have in the world described by thermodynamics, a world of ever-increasing disorder?[6]

Prigogine, who knows quite well that theories at the molecular level are not applicable to living systems, such as a living cell, stresses this problem:

The problem of biological order involves the transition from the molecular activity to the super- molecular order of the cell. This problem is far from being solved.[7]

This is the point most recently arrived at by the chaos theory and related speculations. No concrete outcome has been attained that would support or verify evolution, or eliminate the contradiction between evolution, law of entropy, and other physical laws.

Despite all these evident facts, evolutionists try to take refuge in simple subterfuges. Plain scientific truths show that living things and the ordered, planned, and complex structures of living things could in no way have come into being by coincidence under normal circumstances. This situation makes it clear that the existence of living beings can only be explained by the intervention of a supernatural power. That supernatural power is the creation of God, who created the entire universe from nothing. Science has proven that evolution is still impossible as far as thermodynamics is concerned and the existence of life has no explanation but Creation.

1   Jeremy Rifkin, *Entropy: A New World View*, New York, Viking Press, 1980, p.6
2   J.H.Rush, *The Dawn of Life*, New York, Signet, 1962, p. 35
3   Roger Lewin, "A Downward Slope to Greater Diversity," *Science*, vol. 217, 24.9.1982, p. 1239
4   George P. Stravropoulos, "The Frontiers and Limits of Science," *American Scientist,* vol. 65, November-December 1977, p.674
5   Jeremy Rifkin, *Entropy: A New World View*, p.55
6   Ilya Prigogine, Isabelle Stengers, *Order Out of Chaos*, New York, Bantam Books, 1984, p. 129
7   Ilya Prigogine, Isabelle Stengers, *Order Out of Chaos*, p. 175

THE INFORMATION IN LIVING
STRUCTURES AND THE DEATH
OF MATERIALISM

Materialist philosophy lies at the basis of the theory of evolution. Materialism rests on the supposition that everything that exists is matter. According to this philosophy, matter has existed since eternity, will continue to exist forever, and there is nothing but matter. In order to provide support for their claim, materialists use a logic called "reductionism." This is the idea that things which are not observable can also be explained by material causes.

To make matters clearer, let us take the example of the human mind. It is evident that the mind cannot be touched or seen. Moreover, it has no centre in the human brain. This situation unavoidably leads us to the conclusion that the mind is a concept beyond matter. Therefore, the being which we refer to as "I," who thinks, loves, gets nervous, worries, takes pleasure or feels pain, is not a material being in the same way as a sofa, a table or a stone.

Materialists, however, claim that mind is "reducible to matter." According to the materialist claim, thinking, loving, worrying and all our mental activities are nothing but chemical reactions taking place between the atoms in the brain. Loving someone is a chemical reaction in some cells in our brain, and fear is another. The famous materialist philosopher **Karl Vogt** stressed this logic with his famous words **"Just as the liver secretes gall, so do our brains secrete thought."**[16] Gall, however, is matter, whereas there is no evidence that thought is.

Reductionism is a logical deduction. However, a logical deduction can be based on solid grounds or on shaky ones. For this reason, the question we need to ask is: **What happens when reductionism**, the basic logic of materialism, **is compared to scientific data?**

19th century materialist scientists and thinkers thought that the answer would be that "science verifies reductionism." 20th century science, however, has revealed a very different picture.

One of the most salient feature of this picture is "information," which is present in nature and can never be reduced to matter.

Matter Cannot Produce Information

We earlier mentioned that there is incredibly comprehensive information contained in the DNA of living things. Something as small as a hundred thousandth of a millimetre across contains a sort of "data bank" that specifies all the physical details of the body of a living thing. Moreover, the body also contains a system that reads this information, interprets it and carries out "production" in line with it. In all living cells, the information in the DNA is "read" by various enzymes, and proteins are produced according to this information. This system makes possible the production of millions of proteins every second, of just the required type for just the places where they are needed in our bodies. In this way, dead eye cells are replaced by living ones, and old blood cells by new ones.

At this point, let us consider the claim of materialism: Is it possible that the information in DNA could be reduced to matter, as materialists suggest? Or, in other words, can it be accepted that DNA is merely a collection of matter, and the information it contains came about as a result of the random interactions of such pieces of matter?

All the scientific research, experiments and observations carried out in the 20th century show that the answer to this question is a definite "No." The director of the German Federal Physics and Technology Institute, Prof. Dr. Werner Gitt has this to say on the issue:

A coding system always entails a nonmaterial intellectual process. A physical matter cannot produce an information code. All experiences show

Matter which contains information is ordered by the possessor of that information. The information in DNA has been designed and created by God, the possessor of matchless intelligence.

that every piece of creative information represents some mental effort and can be traced to a personal idea-giver who exercised his own free will, and who is endowed with an intelligent mind.... **There is no known law of nature, no known process and no known sequence of events which can cause information to originate by itself in matter...**[17]

Werner Gitt's words summarise the conclusions of **"information theory,"** which has been developed in the last 50 years and is accepted as a part of thermodynamics. Information theory investigates the origin and nature of the information in the universe. The conclusion reached by the information theoreticians as a result of long studies is that **"Information is something different from matter. It can never be reduced to matter.** The origin of information and physical matter must be investigated separately."

For instance, let us think of the source of a book. A book consists of paper, ink, and the information it contains. Paper and ink are material elements. Their source is again matter: Paper is made of cellulose, and ink of certain chemicals. However, the information in the book is nonmaterial and cannot have a material source. The source of the information in each book is the mind of the person who wrote it.

Moreover, this mind determines how paper and ink will be used. A book initially forms in the mind of the writer. The writer builds a chain of logic in his mind, and orders his sentences. As a second step, he puts them into a material form, which is to say that he translates the information in his mind into letters, using a pen, a typewriter or a computer. Later, these letters are printed in a publishing house and take the shape of a book made up of paper and ink.

We can therefore state this general conclusion: "If physical matter contains information, then that matter must have been designed by a mind that possessed the information in question. First there is the mind. That mind translates the information it possesses into matter, which constitutes the act of design."

The Origin of the Information in Nature

When we apply this scientific definition of information to nature, a very important result ensues. This is because nature overflows with an immense body of information (as, for example, in the case of DNA), and since this information cannot be reduced to matter, it therefore comes from a source beyond matter.

One of the foremost advocates of the theory of evolution, George C. Williams, admits this reality, which most materialists and evolutionists are reluctant to see. Williams has strongly defended materialism for years, but in an article he wrote in 1995, he states the incorrectness of the materialist (reductionist) approach which holds everything is matter:

> Evolutionary biologists have failed to realize that they work with two more or less incommensurable domains: that of information and that of matter. These two domains will never be brought together in any kind of the sense usually implied by the term "reductionism.." The gene is a package of information, not an object... In biology, when you're talking about things like genes and genotypes and gene pools, you're talking about information, not physical objective reality... **This dearth of shared descriptors makes matter and information two separate domains of existence, which have to be discussed separately, in their own terms.**[18]

Therefore, contrary to the supposition of materialists, the source of the information in nature cannot be matter itself. The source of information is not matter but a superior Wisdom beyond matter. This Wisdom existed prior to matter. Matter was brought into existence, given form, and organised by Him.

APE–MAN SIMILARITY
IS A TALE!

*The completion of the human's gene map today does not yield
the result that man and ape are relatives. One need not be deceived
by evolutionists' attempts to exploit this new scientific development
just as they have done with all others.*

As we know, the recent completion of the human gene map within the scope of the **Human Genome Project** was a very important scientific advance. However, some results of this project are being distorted in some evolutionist publications. It is claimed that **the chimpanzee genes bear a 98% similarity to human genes** and this is promoted as evidence for the claim that apes are related to humans, thus bearing out the theory of evolution. In truth, this is a "fake" piece of evidence put forward by evolutionists who take advantage of the lack of knowledge about this subject in society.

98 % Similarity Claim is Misleading Propaganda

First, it should be stated that the concept of **98% similarity between human and chimpanzee DNA** frequently advanced by evolutionists **is deceptive**.

In order to claim that the genetic make-up of man and chimpanzee have a 98% similarity, the genome of the chimpanzee also has to be mapped, just like that of man, the two have to be compared, and the result of this comparison has to be obtained. However, no such result is available, because so far, only the human gene has been mapped. No such research has yet been done on the chimpanzee.

In reality, the 98% similarity between human and chimpanzee genes, which now and then enters the agenda, is a propaganda-oriented slogan deliberately invented years ago. This similarity is an extraordinarily exaggerated generalisation grounded on the similarity in the amino acid sequences of **some 30-40 basic proteins** present in man and the chimpanzee. A sequence analysis has been made using a method named "DNA hybridisation" on the DNA sequences that are correlated with these proteins and only that limited number of proteins has been compared.

However, there are about one hundred thousand genes, and therefore one hundred thousand proteins encoded by these genes in humans. For that reason, **there is no scientific basis for claiming that all the genes of man and ape are 98% similar just because of the similarity in 40 out of 100,000 proteins.**

Moreover, the DNA comparison carried out on these 40 proteins is also controversial. This comparison was made in 1987 by two biologists named Sibley and Ahlquist and published in the *Journal of Molecular Evolution*.[19] However, another scientist named Sarich, who examined the data obtained by these two scientists, concluded that **the reliability of the method they used is controversial and that the data has been exaggeratedly interpreted.**[20]

Research in modern laboratories has revealed that all evolutionist claims about the roots of life are nothing but fairy stories.

Human DNA is also Similar to that of the Worm, Mosquito and Chicken!

Moreover, the above-mentioned basic proteins are common vital molecules present in various other living things. The structure of the same kinds of proteins present not only in the chimpanzee, but also in completely different living creatures, is very similar to that in humans.

For example, genetic analyses published in *New Scientist* have revealed a **75 % similarity between the DNAs of nematode worms and man.**[21] This definitely does not mean that there is only a 25% difference between man and these worms! According to the family tree made by evolutionists, the Chordata phylum, in which man is included, and the Nematoda phylum were different from each other even 530 million years ago.

On the other hand, in another finding which also appeared in the media, it was stated that **the comparisons carried out between the genes of fruit flies belonging to the Drosophila species and human genes yielded a similarity of 60%.**[22]

In another case, analyses done on certain proteins show man as closely linked to some very different living things. In a survey carried out

A headline from a popular newspaper in Turkey: "It is discovered that we are relatives with flies!". The sub-heading reads: "A fruit fly, whose genetic code has been mapped, surprised scientists. The genes of the fly are similar to those of man's by 60%." This is an example of news stories about genetic similarities. Stories such as this are examples of attempts to portray the concept of genetic similarity as evidence for the theory of evolution. However, genetic similarity is nothing of the kind.

by researchers in Cambridge University, some proteins of land-dwelling animals were compared. Amazingly, in nearly all samples, **human beings and chickens were paired as the closest relatives.** The next closest relative was the crocodile.[23]

Another example used by evolutionists on "the genetic similarity between man and ape," **is the presence of 48 chromosomes in chimpanzees and gorillas versus 46 chromosomes in man.** Evolutionists regard the closeness of the number of chromosomes as indication of an evolutionary relationship. However, if this logic used by evolutionists were valid, then man would have an even closer relative than the chimpanzee: **"the potato"! Because the number of chromosomes in potatoes is the same as that of man: 46**

These examples confirm that the concept of genetic similarity does not constitute evidence for the theory of evolution. This is because the genetic similarities are not in line with the alleged evolutionary schemes, and on the contrary, yield completely opposite results.

Genetic Similarities Upset the "Evolution Scheme" that is Sought to be Constituted

Unsurprisingly, when the issue is evaluated as a whole, it is seen that the subject of "bio-chemical similarities" does not constitute evidence for evolution, but rather leaves the theory in the lurch. Dr. Christian Schwabe, a biochemistry researcher from the Medical Faculty of South Carolina University, is an evolutionist scientist who has spent years searching for evidence for evolution in the molecular domain. In particular he carried out research on insulin and relaxin-type proteins and tried to establish evolutionary relationships between living beings. However, he had to confess many times that he could not find any evidence for evolution at any point in his studies. In an article published in a scientific journal, he said;

> Molecular evolution is about to be accepted as a method superior to palaeontology for the discovery of evolutionary relationships. As a molecular evolutionist I should be elated. **Instead it seems disconcerting that many exceptions exist to the orderly progression of species as determined by molecular homologies**; so many in fact that I think the exception, the quirks, may carry the more important message.[24]

Based on the recent findings obtained in the field of molecular biology, the renowned biochemist Prof. Michael Denton made the following comments;

> Each class at molecular level is unique, isolated and unlinked by intermediates. Thus, molecules, like fossils, have failed to provide the elusive intermediates so long sought by evolutionary biology... **At a molecular level, no organism is "ancestral" or "primitive" or "advanced" compared with its relatives...** There is little doubt that if this molecular evidence had been available a century ago... the idea of organic evolution might never have been accepted.[25]

Similarities are not Evidence for Evolution but for Creation

It is surely natural for the human body to bear some molecular similarities to other living beings, because they all are made up of the same molecules, they all use the same water and atmosphere, and they all consume foods consisting of the same molecules. Certainly, their metabolisms and therefore genetic make-ups would resemble one another. This, however, is not evidence that they evolved from a common ancestor.

This **"common material" is not the result of an evolution but of "common design,"** that is, their being created upon the same plan.

It is possible to explain this point with an example: all construction in the world is done with similar materials (brick, iron, cement, etc.). This, however, does not mean that these buildings "evolved" from each other.

They are constructed separately by using common materials. The same holds for living beings as well.

Life did not originate as the result of unconscious coincidences as evolution claims, but as the result of the creation of God, the Almighty, the possessor of infinite knowledge and wisdom.

He is the Originator of the heavens and the earth. How could He have a son when He has no wife? He created all things and He has knowledge of all things. That is God, your Lord. There is no deity but Him, the Creator of everything. So worship Him. He is responsible for everything. (Qur'an, 6:101-102)

Conclusion

In addition to all the information we have detailed so far, we think it would be helpful to emphasize another fact.

Other than the superficial similarity between them, apes are no closer to human beings than other animals. Moreover, when intelligence is used as a point of comparison, the bee, which produces the geometrical wonder of the honeycomb, or the spider, which produces the engineering wonder of the web, are closer to man than the ape. We can even say that they are superior in some aspects.

Between man and ape, however, there is a tremendous gap, never to be closed by fairy stories. After all, an ape is an animal no different from a horse or a dog in terms of consciousness. Man, however, is a being who has consciousness and will, who can think, talk, reason, decide, and judge. All these qualities are functions of the "spirit" he possesses. The most important difference that causes this huge gap between man and other living beings is this "spirit." No physical resemblance can close this gap between man and other living beings. The only being that has "spirit" in nature is man.

In the Qur'an, this superior quality which man possesses and which differentiates him from other living things is referred to as follows:

Then He formed him and breathed His Spirit into him and gave you hearing, sight and hearts. What little thanks you show! (Qur'an, 32:9)

DARWINIST–MATERIALIST MISCONCEPTIONS ABOUT THE HUMAN GENOME PROJECT

With the announcement of the latest point arrived at in the Human Genome Project, some publishing organs have started to deliver misleading messages and misinform the public, so that the impasse the theory of evolution has reached may not be further revealed.

Earlier, we mentioned the misleading messages evolutionists gave about "genetic similarities" and made it clear that these are subjective interpretations which do not provide any evidence for the theory of evolution. Another subject, which is mostly promoted and highlighted with different slogans and headlines by the Darwinist–Materialist press, is the claim that the discovery of the gene map suggests that the fate decreed by God can be challenged. This is a great misconception and deception put forward by certain circles. The headlines recently appearing in the printed press and statements made in the course of discussions on television programs give the impression of a stealthy indoctrination. It is a great mistake to present the information on the human genome project accompanied by messages like "Man will no longer be defeated by his destiny." For in truth, the mapping of the human genes has no relevance whatsoever to the flow of man's fate. The production of the human gene map will certainly not change the shape of man's destiny, because that too has been pre-destined.

The Flow of Fate Cannot be Changed

Destiny is God's perfect knowledge of all events, past or future, as a single moment. God already knows events that have not yet been experienced. A large number of people do not understand how God can know what will happen in the future, in other words the reality of destiny. However, "events not yet experienced" are only so for us. All those events, the results of which we describe as "unknown," are only "unknown" to us. God, who possesses infinite knowledge, is not bound by time and space. In any case, it was He who created time and space. For this reason, past, future, and present are all the same to God; for Him everything has already taken place and finished. Everything that we are experiencing now, and will experience in the future, is already over and done with in the sight of God. At the appropriate time, all people witness the destiny that God has prepared for them.

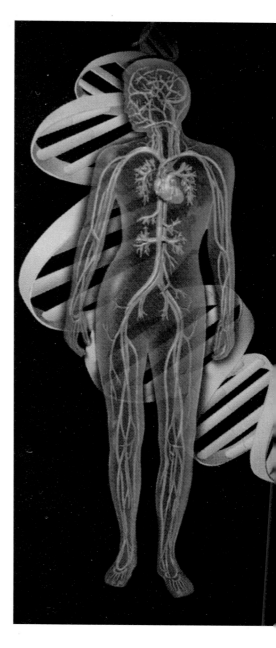

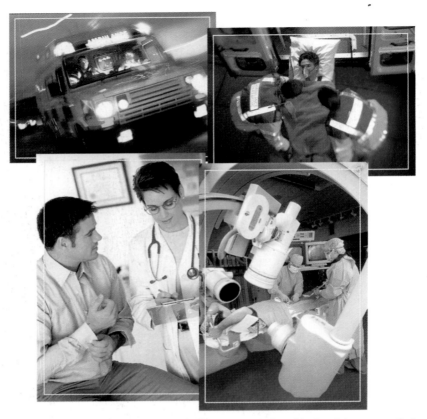

Everything that happens in someone's life: unexpected accidents, sickness, medical treatment and recovery, everything that seems good or bad, happens in the context of the destiny set out by God. Whether the person in the picture will recover or not is determined right from the moment he falls sick. In the same way, the hospital he will be treated in, how long he will stay there and what kind of treatment he will receive are all predetermined in the sight of God. If this person is one day restored to health by new technology, that is also his destiny. It is God who has created and knows everything.

In the same way that someone who picks up a film spool can see the beginning, the end and everything in between as a single whole, so God knows everything about the human beings He has created. God, who knows everything as a single instant, reveals His power to us by creating infinity, or infinitely long time, in a single moment, that is, in infinitely short time.

God created all people past and present in the knowledge of every detail of their lives. Everything that a person will experience, that seems good or bad to him, happens within the knowledge of God. The Sura An'am reveals that everything that happens in the world, be it great or small, happens by the will of God:

> **The keys of the Unseen are in His possession. No one knows them but Him. He knows everything on the land and in the sea. No leaf falls without His knowing it. There is no seed in the darkness of the earth, and nothing moist or dry which is not in a Clear Book.** (Qur'an, 6:59)

This is true for everyone and every event. It is neither possible for anyone to alter the destiny that God has prepared for him, nor to bring about any change in the flow of events. For instance, God has created everyone with a certain lifetime and everyone's moment of death is determined as to its location, time and form in the sight of God. For instance, a disease a person will suffer from has been predestined billions of years ago before his birth. Whether or not he will recover from that sickness has been decided in his fate by God. Even the doctors, nurses, hospital, medicines and methods of treatment that will be the vehicles for his recovery have been written in advance in the sight of God. For that reason, the fact that someone recovers does not mean he has cheated his fate, but that his recovery was part of that same fate.

If, in the years to come, someone's lifetime is extended with timely interventions in the genes, this would not mean that this event defeated that person's destiny. It simply means the following: God gave this man a long life and He made the completion of gene mapping a means for his life to be long. The discovery of the gene map, that person's living in that period and that person's life being extended by scientific means are all his destiny. All is determined in the sight of God before this person is born into the world.

Similarly, someone whose fatal sickness is cured through the discoveries made within the scope of this project has again not changed his destiny. That is because it is this person's destiny to recover from this illness by means of this project. Consequently, completion of the human genome project and the fact that man will be able to intervene in the genetic make-up, do not mean confronting the destiny created by God. On the contrary, in this way, mankind follows the developments created for it by God, and explores and benefits from the information created by God. If man lives 120 years thanks to these scientific developments, this is surely a lifetime decreed for him by God, that is why he lives so long.

God reveals in one verse that every person's life is set out in a book in His sight:

> God created you from dust and then from a drop of sperm and then made you into pairs. No female becomes pregnant or gives birth except with His knowledge. And no living thing lives long or has its life cut short without that being in a Book. That is easy for God. (Qur'an, 35:11)

A student who fails university entrance exams for years before getting in to the department he wants, a businessman who saves his company from bankruptcy, people who escape a plane hijacking at the last moment, and others doing similar things are all living out their destinies. None of them can change that destiny, nor does anyone else have the power to change their destiny for them.

In brief, utterances like "I cheated my fate," "I changed my destiny" or "I intervened in my destiny" are the consequence of ignorance caused by not knowing the facts about fate. On the other hand, a person's using these expressions is also predestined; how, when and under which conditions he will make these statements are all determined in the sight of God. It is God who knows all.

God informed us that everything is recorded in a clear book in His sight. We live what is written in that book, no more and no less.

> Those who disbelieve say, "The Hour will never come." Say: "Yes, by my Lord, it certainly will come!" He is the Knower of the Unseen, whom not even the weight of the smallest particle eludes, either in the heavens or in the earth; nor is there anything smaller or larger than that which is not recorded in a Clear Book. (Qur'an, 34:3)

> Nothing occurs, either in the earth or in yourselves, without its being in a Book before We make it happen. That is something easy for God. (Qur'an, 57:22)

Cloning a Human Being or Any Other Living Being is Not Creating

In some publications, it has been alleged that by the advancement of the science of genetics, human beings would be cloned and therefore, human beings would create human beings. This, too, is a very distorted and farfetched piece of logic. Creating means to bring something into being from nothingness, and this act is peculiar to God alone. The formation of the identical copy of a living being by copying genetic information does not mean that this living being has been created. When a man or any other living being is cloned, the cells of a living being are taken and copied. However, never has a single living cell been created from nothingness by man. The research conducted on this subject has been stopped: it was all inconclusive.

Consequently, the discovery of the human genetic make-up by no means implies man's challenge to his destiny, and it never can. Every incident, every act of speech and development are all predetermined in the sight of God according to a certain destiny. So are technological advances, scientific developments and the innovations they will introduce. God is All-Knowing, and All-Encompassing. The fact that everything, big or small, takes places within the knowledge of God is stated in the Qur'an as follows:

> **You do not engage in any matter or recite any of the Qur'an or do any action without Our witnessing you while you are occupied with it. Not even the smallest speck eludes your Lord, either on earth or in heaven. Nor is there anything smaller than that, or larger, which is not in a Clear Book.**
> (Qur'an, 10:61)

THE LATEST FOSSIL CLAIM
OF THE THEORY OF EVOLUTION HAS
ALSO BECOME HISTORY

The theory of evolution has met a crushing defeat in palaeontology as well as in biochemical topics such as genes, DNA and the cell systems. Fossils demonstrate that living species did not evolve from each other, but were created separately with their individual specific characteristics.

According to the theory of evolution, all living species evolved from one another. A previously-existing species turned into another species over time and all species came into being in this manner. According to the theory, this transformation has been over a very long period of hundreds of millions of years and proceeded gradually.

In that case, numerous **"intermediary species"** should have originated and lived within this long alleged transformation period.

For instance, some half-fish/half-reptiles should have lived in the past which had acquired some reptilian traits in addition to the fish traits they already had. Or some reptile-birds should have originated which had acquired some bird traits in addition to the reptilian traits they already had. Since they were in a transitory period, they had to be crippled, deficient, and defective living beings. Evolutionists refer to these theoretical creatures, which they believe to have lived in the past, as **"transitional forms."**

If such animals had really existed in the past, there should be millions and even billions of them in number and variety. Darwinism is shattered right at this point, because there is not a single trace of these imaginary "intermediate transitional forms."

But Will It Fly?

Scientists Say Fossils From China Prove Dinosaur-to-Bird Link

In our other studies on the invalidity of the theory of evolution, we had explained that Arhaeopteryx is not a living being in between bird-dinosaur, but an extinct bird species which could fly just like the modern birds. Despite this fact, some evolutionist publications still accepted Archaeopteryx as the "primitive ancestor of birds" and repeat the tale of "dinosaurs are the ancestors of birds". Above is seen misleading coverage in *New Scientist* and *National Geographic* about Archaeopteryx. Finally, however, truths have been revealed and even evolutionist publications had to admit the collapse of the Archaeopteryx legend.

Imaginary
Archaeopteryx
picture

This fact has been known for a long time. Yet evolutionists speculated on a few fossils, trying to present them as "intermediate transitional forms" and comforted themselves saying, "only a few intermediate forms have been found so far, but in the future all of them will be unearthed." The most important fossil presented as an intermediate form was a 150-million-year-old extinct bird fossil called Archaeopteryx. Evolutionists claimed that this bird had reptilian traits. Despite the fact that their claims have been refuted one by one and that it has been proved that Archaeopteryx was not an intermediate transitional form but a flying bird species, they desperately embraced this last fossil they had.

"Fossil Discovery Threatens Theory of Birds' Evolution"

At last, a fossil discovered during recent years, definitely overthrew the claims of evolutionists. As quoted from the evolutionist sources, a fossil was discovered which revealed that the ancient ancestor of birds was not a dinosaur or any other living being but a bird.

News about this discovery first appeared in the world media on June 23, 2000. The *New York Times* carried the headline **"Fossil Discovery Threatens Theory of Birds' Evolution."** This article was about a bird which was recently unearthed in the Middle East. Prominent scientific journals such as *Science* and *Nature* and the world-renowned TV network of the BBC announced the recent developments as follows: "It has been discovered that the fossil, which was unearthed in the Middle East and estimated to have lived 220 million years ago, is covered with feathers, has a wishbone just like Archaeopteryx and modern birds do, and there are hollow shafts in its feathers. **THIS INVALIDATES THE CLAIMS**

Fossil Discovery Threatens Theory of Birds' Evolution

By JOHN NOBLE WILFORD

Scientists have discovered fossil evidence of the oldest known feathered animal, a small reptile that probably glided among the trees 75 million years before the earliest known bird, and they say this challenges the widely held theory that birds evolved from dinosaurs.

The Ancestor of Birds Proved to be A Bird: A news item based on a news that appeared in *New York Times* on June 23, 2000 headlined "Fossil Discovery Threatens Theory of Birds' Evolution".

Challenge to a Theory of Birds' Evolution

Continued From Page A1

...lease by Oregon State University in Corvallis, one of several universities from which researchers were drawn, members of the discovery team threw down the gauntlet in their dispute with other paleontologists who favor a direct evolutionary link between dinosaurs and birds.

While the new fossil evidence does not conclusively establish that Longisquama was an ancestor of flying birds, John A. Ruben of Oregon State said, it would have lived in the right time and had the right physical structure to have been an ancestor — and it was earlier than a dinosaur...

Mark A. Norell, a paleontologist at the American Museum of Natural History in New York and a leading exponent of a dinosaurian ancestry of birds, said he was not ready to concede that the fossil impressions are of true feathers.

"Even if these turn out to be feathers, they have not established that Longisquama is ancestral to modern birds," Dr. Norell said.

The discovery ruffling paleontology's feathers was made by scientists from the University of Kansas, the Russian Academy of Sciences, the University of North Carolina at Chapel Hill, the City University of

Other paleontologists and ornithologists were called in for a look. Alan Feduccia of the University of North Carolina, author of "The Origin and Evolution of Birds" (Yale University Press), was struck by the hollow shaft covered by a sheath, a characteristic of bird feathers.

"This is a dramatic finding," Dr. Feduccia said. "Everything about the feather points to aerodynamic structure, indicating that the initial function of feathers was in an aerodynamic context."

A point of contention in the dinosaur-bird debate centers on the initial function of feathers. Dinosaur partisans argue that when some dinosaurs became warm-blooded they...

THAT ARCHAEOPTERYX IS THE ANCESTOR OF BIRDS, because the fossil discovered is 75 million years older than Archaeopteryx. This means that **A REAL BIRD WITH ALL ITS CHARACTERISTIC FEATURES ALREADY EXISTED 75 MILLION YEARS BEFORE THE CREATURE WHICH WAS ALLEGED TO BE THE ANCESTOR OF BIRDS.**"

A Milestone in the History of the Palaeontology

The admission by evolutionists themselves that Archaeopteryx is not an "intermediate transitional form" serving as evidence for evolution is an important milestone in the history of palaeontology. This is because for about 150 years, Archaeopteryx has continued to be the most prominent among the very few so-called "intermediate transitional forms" evolutionists could advance. However, this door of escape is also closed now, and the world of palaeontology has had to face the plain truth that **there is not even a single fossil which can provide evidence for evolution**.

The outcomes are evident. *The New York Times* also accepted that fact and ran the headline "Fossil Discovery Threatens Theory of Birds' Evolution." That is true. Indeed, the ancestor of birds was a bird. The ancestor of fish was a fish, the ancestor of horses was a horse, the ancestor of kangaroos was a kangaroo and the ancestor of man was a man. In other words, **all different classes of living beings emerged in the perfect and specific forms they have today. In other words, they were created by God.**

The conservative resistance evolutionists show towards this evident fact has now lost its last cornerstone.

They said "Glory be to You!

We have no knowledge except what

You have taught us. You are the

All-Knowing, the All-Wise."

(Quran, 2:32)

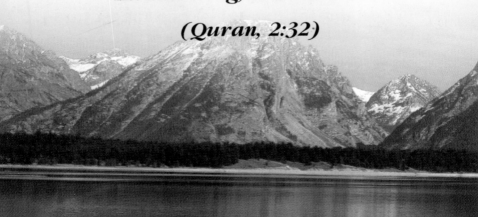

NOTES

1 Michael Denton. *Evolution: A Theory in Crisis*. London: Burnett Books, 1985, p. 334

2 Prof. Dr. Ali Demirsoy, *Kalıtım ve Evrim*, p.158

3 Frank B. Salisbury, *"Doubts About The Modern Synthetic Theory of Evolution,"* p. 336

4 Francis Crick, *Life Itself: It's Origin and Nature*, New York, Simon & Schuster, 1981, p. 88

5 Orgel, Leslie E, "Darwinism at the Very Beginning of Life," *New Scientist*, vol.94 (April 15, 1982), p.151

6 Pierre-P Grassé, *Evolution of Living Organisms*, New York: Academic Press, 1977, p. 103

7 Douglas R. Hofstadter, Gödel, Escher, *Bach: An Eternal Golden Braid*, New York: Vintage Books, 1980, p. 548

8 Leslie E. Orgel, "The Origin of Life on Earth," *Scientific American*, Vol.271, October 1994, p. 78

9 Haskins, Caryl P., "Advances and Challenges in Science in 1970," *American Scientist*, vol.59 (May/June 1971), p.305)

10 Michael Denton, *Evolution: A Theory in Crisis*, London: Burnett Books, 1985, p. 351

11 John Horgan, "In the Beginning," *Scientific American*, Vol. 264, February 1991, p. 119

12 G.F. Joyce, L. E. Orgel, *"Prospects for Understanding the Origin of the RNA World,"* In the RNA World, New York: Cold Spring Harbor Laboratory Press, 1993, p. 13

13 Jacques Monod, *Chance and Necessity*, New York: 1971, p.143

14 Leslie E. Orgel, "The Origin of Life on the Earth," *Scientific American*, October 1994, Cilt 271, p. 78

15 Chandra Wickramasinghe, *Interview in London Daily Express*, 14 August 1981

16 *Encyclopædia Britannica*, "Modern Materialism"

17 Werner Gitt. *In the Beginning Was Information*. CLV, Bielefeld, Germany, p. 107, 141

18 George C. Williams. *The Third Culture: Beyond the Scientific Revolution*. (ed. John Brockman). New York, Simon & Schuster, 1995. p. 42-43

19 *Journal of Molecular Evolution*, vol. 26, p. 99-121

20 Sarich et al. 1989. *Cladistics* 5:3-32

21 *New Scientist*, 15 May 1999, p. 27

22 http://news.bbc.co.uk/1/hi/sci/tech/specials/washington-2000/647139.stm

23 *New Scientist*, c. 103, 16 August 1984, p. 19

24 Christian Schwabe, "On the Validity of Molecular Evolution," *Trends in Biochemical Sciences*, c. 11, July 1986

25 Michael Denton. *Evolution: A Theory in Crisis*. London: Burnett Books, 1985, p. 290-9

A study that examines and seeks to remind us of the basic moral principles of the Qur'an, particularly those that are most likely to be forgotten or neglected at times.

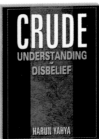

God, in the Qur'an, calls the culture of people who are not subject to the religion of God "ignorance." Only a comparison of this culture with the moral structure of the Qur'an can reveal its crude nature. The purpose of this book is to display the extent of the "crude understanding" of ignorant societies.

The Qur'an has been revealed to us so that we may read and ponder it. Unfortunately, current attitudes towards religion in society today discourage people from pondering the Qur'an. The primary duty of a Muslim is to thoroughly learn the book of God for it was revealed to people by their sole Lord as a "guidance to those who believe" (Surat al-Baqara, 2). Basic Concepts in the Qur'an is a useful resource prepared as a guide on this subject.

One of the principal deceptions that impels people into delinquency and makes them pursue their own desires is their heedlessness of death. Both human beings and the universe they live in are mortal. What awaits the disbelievers in the next world is more dreadful: the eternal wrath of hell. This book, based on the verses of the Qur'an, makes a detailed depiction of the moment of death, the day of judgement, and the penalties in hell, and it sounds a warning about the great danger facing us.

Children's Books

These books, which are prepared for kids, are about the miraculous characteristics of the living things on the earth. Full colour and written in a clear style, these books give your children the opportunity to get to know God and His perfect artistry in creation. The first books of this series are *The World of Our Little Friends The Ants* and *Honeybees That Build Perfect Combs*.

Medicine and biology books say that we owe our senses of smell and taste to our nose, tongue and brain. It is true that we smell and taste with the help of these organs. But to whom do we owe our nose and brain? The purpose of this book is to reveal the proofs of creation in these systems, thus helping the reader to contemplate the boundless knowledge and power of God, and to have a full grasp of His infinite blessings.

Though we witness the miracle in God's Creation all around us we fail to think deeply about them. This book helps to enhance our faith in the Almighty and shows the invalidity of perverted theories concerning life. Highly informative and sincere in style, this book can be enjoyed by both children and grown-ups. The magnificent pictures and illustrations enhance the worth of this book.

There are questions about religion that people seek answers to and hope to be enlightened in the best way. However in most cases, people base their opinions on hearsay rather than acquiring them from the real source of religion: the Qur'an. In these book, you will find the most accurate answers to all the questions you seek answers for and learn your responsibilities towards your Creator. .

The most serious mistake a man makes is not pondering. It is not possible to find the truth unless one thinks about basic questions such as "How and why am I here?", "Who created me?", or "Where am I going?." Failing to do so, one becomes trapped in the vicious circle of daily life and turns into a selfish creature caring only for himself. Ever Thought About the Truth? summons people to think on such basic questions and to discover the real meaning of life.

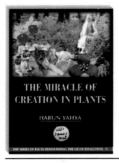

The purpose of this book is to display the miraculous features of plants and hence to make people see "the creation miracle" in things -they often encounter in the flow of their daily lives and sidestep.

This book opens new horizons on these issues for people who, throughout their lives, -think only about their own needs and hence fail to see the evidence of God's existence. Reading and understanding this book will be an important step in coming to an understanding of one's Creator.

This book reveals the "miracle in the eye" In it, you will find a description of a perfect system and the story of the unbelievable events taking place behind the hundreds of eyes we see each day... As in all the books of this series, this one discusses the theory of evolution in detail and the collapse of that theory is proven once more. When you read the book, you will see how right Darwin was when he said "The thought of the eye makes me cold all over."

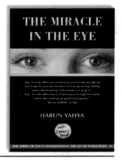

The evidence of God's creation is present everywhere in the universe. A person comes across many of these proofs in the course of his daily life. In every creature there are great mysteries to be pondered. Ants, the millimetric-sized animals that we frequently come across but don't care much about have an excellent ability for organization and specialization that is not to be matched by any other being on earth. These aspects of ants create in one a great admiration for God's superior power and unmatched creation.

Termites, which are the subject matter of this book, are a species of insect that we are not accustomed to see around us. Though partly similar to ants in their lives and appeareances, termites have very different features and abilities. A book on termites may be very surprising for some people. They may think that there would not be much to tell about a little insect. When you read about the characteristics of termites, however, you will see that this idea is totally wrong. This insect, about which little is known, and which is mostly brushed aside, is equipped with many miraculous features that will open up a new horizon of thought, revealing God's matchless creation.